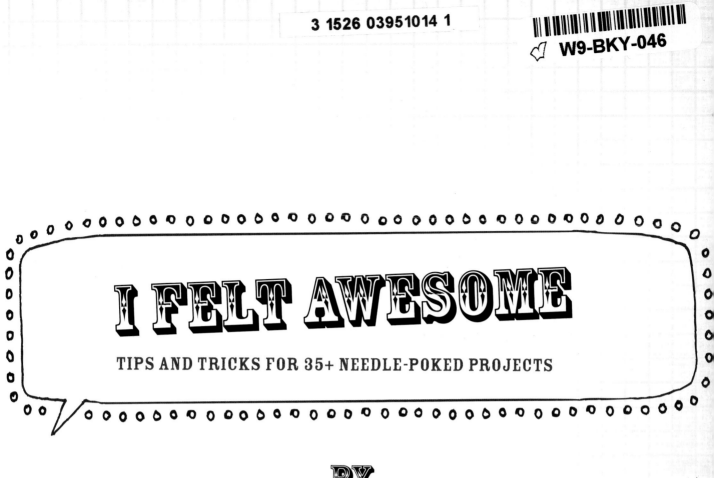

# I FELT AWESOME

## TIPS AND TRICKS FOR 35+ NEEDLE-POKED PROJECTS

### BY
### MOXIE

**NORTH LIGHT BOOKS**
Cincinnati, Ohio

www.fwmedia.com

14 13 12 11 10 5 4 3 2 1

DISTRIBUTED IN CANADA BY FRASER DIRECT
100 Armstrong Avenue
Georgetown, ON, Canada L7G 5S4
Tel: (905) 877-4411

DISTRIBUTED IN THE U.K. AND EUROPE BY F+W MEDIA INTERNATIONAL
Brunel House, Newton Abbot, Devon, TQ12 4PU, England
Tel: (+44) 1626 323200, Fax: (+44) 1626 323319
Email: postmaster@davidandcharles.co.uk

DISTRIBUTED IN AUSTRALIA BY CAPRICORN LINK
P.O. Box 704, S. Windsor NSW, 2756 Australia
Tel: (02) 4577-3555

Library of Congress Cataloging in Publication Data
Moxie.
  I felt awesome : tips and tricks for 35+ needle-poked projects / by Moxie.
      p. cm.
  Includes index.
  ISBN 978-1-60061-792-8 (pbk. : alk. paper)
  1. Felting. 2. Felt work.  I. Title.
  TT849.5.M69 2010
  746'.0463--dc22
                            2010017442

Edited by Julie Hollyday
Designed by Corrie Schaffeld and Michelle Thompson
Production coordinated by Greg Nock
Photography by Christine Polomsky
Illustrations by Rob Warnick
Template illustrations by Demian Parker

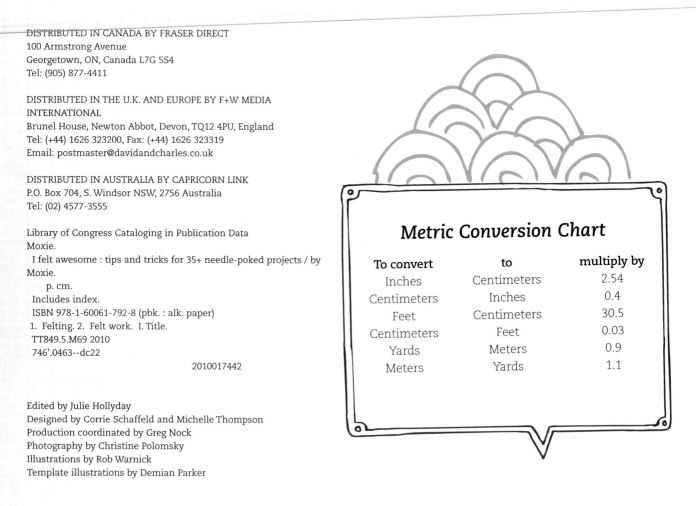

## Metric Conversion Chart

| To convert | to | multiply by |
|---|---|---|
| Inches | Centimeters | 2.54 |
| Centimeters | Inches | 0.4 |
| Feet | Centimeters | 30.5 |
| Centimeters | Feet | 0.03 |
| Yards | Meters | 0.9 |
| Meters | Yards | 1.1 |

# DEDICATION

For my husband: Hey Paul, do you remember that time I was lost in the wilderness, surrounded by poisonous creatures and mysterious fog and I thought I'd be there for all time, but then you strolled into the chaos and took my hand and led me out of peril and into your life? I may have forgotten to say thanks. Also, your caboose looked really hot in those pants.

# ACKNOWLEDGEMENTS

## WITHOUT THESE PEOPLE, THERE WOULD BE NO BOOK:
Kristen Rask, Nikola Davidson, Paul Palinkas, Snafu and Hermano, Nancy Stetson, Layne Goldsmith, Demian Parker and Brookelynn Morris.

## MANY THANKS TO:
Rachel J. Lieberman, LeAnne Laux-Bachand, Marlo Miyashiro, Shellie Gravitt, Sandra Kurland, Lisa Black, Lou Kipilman, Quincy, M.E., Becky Stern, Natalie Zee Drieu, Rachel Hobson Nick Hubbard and all the naked sheep whose wool has been shorn in the name of art.

## UNENDING GRATITUDE TO:
Julie Hollyday, Christine Polomsky, Corrie Schaffeld, Michelle Thompson, Tonia Davenport and all the fine folks at F+W Media for your work, patience and kindness.

## NO THANKS TO:
My parents, Gene and Kerin Lieberman. I know you both would have enjoyed this book if only you had managed to stay alive long enough to see it. Pretty lame, dudes. But for real, I miss you.

# TABLE OF CONTENTS

# INTRODUCTION

I owe you an apology. Sure, we've only just met, but please understand how deeply sorry I am.

You picked up this book just a moment ago, but you are teetering on the brink of a serious needle felting addiction. You think you're casually browsing a craft book, receiving an apology from an author you've only just met, but this is how it starts. Pretty soon, you're going to flip through the pages of this book. "Just browsing," you'll call it. You're going to see how fuzzy and colorful the wool looks, and how intriguing the felting needles are. Your heart's gonna start beating a little faster and your throat will get a little dry.

Flip a few more pages and you'll see how simple the concept of needle felting is and how many amazing things you can learn to make. Next thing you know, you'll be at home with this book and your supplies, ready to begin. This, my poor dear friend, is the point of no return. Once you poke the needle into the fiber and feel the satisfaction of turning wool into flat and 3D accessories, toys and sculptures, you'll never be able to stop. I know because, my name is Moxie, and I'm a felt-aholic.

Needle felting is a fun, creative and simple craft with unequaled versatility. Because the materials are relatively clean and completely portable, needle felting is a great lap activity that you can take pretty much anywhere you feel like making stuff. The materials won't bust your crafting budget and the tools can be re-used for dozens of projects.

Made without sewing or weaving, felt is a matted fabric and is the oldest textile known to humankind. The first felt was created by agitating natural wool fiber using soapy water, causing the individual fibers to interlock. Needle, or dry felting, is the process of turning wool fiber into felt using sharp, barbed needles that make the wool fibers attach to each other. (Hundreds of these needles in machines make the felt you buy at the craft store.) Basically, these special needles do the same job the water and soap can do.

If you've seen or tried needle felting before, you'll probably notice that the instructions in this book are a little different. That's because I'm a self-taught felter, a teacher of felting and a believer in open-ended learning; the techniques and tricks in this book are the product of all my hands-on investigation. I encourage you to mix and match techniques that you learn here and experiment with moves of your own.

That's the best part about needle felting: I never stop learning new things about what it can do. That's probably why it never gets boring, I never want to put it down, and I'm now spreading the addiction on to you.

I really am very sorry.

# TOOLS

One of the great things about felting is that you don't have to buy lots of expensive and confusing equipment. Here are the essentials you'll need to complete the projects in this book and beyond.

## FELTING NEEDLES

So simple, so elegant, so sharp; felting needles are where the magic comes from. You can find them in lots of sizes and several variations, but you can always count on the 38-gauge star needle to see you through your projects. If you absolutely crave diversity, I recommend the 40-gauge triangle needle for help with finer details.

## MULTI-NEEDLE TOOLS

When you make flat felt or large sculptures, multi-needle tools will help you cover more surface area as you poke. A tool with four needles is great for beginners, but you can find tools with more needles, too. Remember, the more needles in your tool, the more careful you need to be.

## FOAM PAD

A foam pad protects your needles and your table or lap. You can use any piece of upholstery foam, scrap foam from packaging, etc. My favorite foam for almost every felting project are foams made from vegetable starch. They have great surface tension and, unlike most other foams, are completely biodegradable.

## DESIGN CENTER

Templates, transfer papers and fabric markers are all helpful when the surface design of your project needs to be just so. I list the specific ones you'll need in the Materials & Tools sections of various projects.

## SCHOOL SUPPLIES

Sometimes you'll want to do some marking and cutting and some other grown-up stuff called "preparation." That's when you'd use pencils, rulers, paper, glue, etc. Again, those are all noted in the projects.

## HARDWARE

A pair of pliers here, a hammer there; whatever it takes to get the job done is what you'll use. Check out the Materials & Tools lists for each project for specifics.

## BONUS TOOLS

Needle felting is fuzzy and sharp. Have the following on hand to help keep sane and healthy.

**Lint Brush**
Fiber artists like you and me often look like we herd Muppets all day. Whether it's a sticky-paper roller or a fabric lint brush, you'll be happy you have it.

**Adhesive Bandages**
Every once in a while, you'll poke yourself. Keep some adhesive bandages in your kit to avoid getting blood on your work. Blood is gross.

Safety

*A felting needle will probably be the sharpest sharp thing you've ever played with. It's not hard to stay safe, and the following tips will help eliminate 90 percent of common felting mishaps:*

- *Always watch your hands while felting. Whenever you look away from your work, stop moving your hands. You may think you can glance up at the TV or your loved ones and poke the needle just one more time, but you are wrong.*

- *Don't felt when you're tired. If you are sleepy, you don't have to go to bed, but you should definitely step away from the felting.*

- *Soft stabs are better than hard jabs. It doesn't take a lot of force to push the needle through the wool. The softer you poke, the less it will hurt if you do happen to miss the work and hit yourself.*

# MATERIALS

The main ingredient you need to make felt is fiber and lots of it. You can make your projects from scratch using nothing but wool, like me, or use some bonus goodies to help the work go faster.

## FIBER STASH

All animal hair can felt, including rabbit, camel, cat and dog ... even yours! Sheep wool is a great go-to fiber. When wool has been combed, cleaned and carded into a loose rope, it's often called roving. In this book, I mostly use Corriedale because it's soft enough to wear against the skin, but coarse enough for 3D felting with ease. Merino is another popular wool, but it's finer and may take a little extra time and effort to sculpt into shapes.

There is no end to the colors, textures and sheen that come from combing, layering and mixing fibers together into beautiful feltable batts. You can find batts that incorporate bamboo silk, cashmere, yarn bits, hemp, light reflective plastic or nylon, recycled sari silk and more, online and in local yarn shops.

## FILLERS

Felting around objects can save you time and keep you sane. You can use Styrofoam, upholstery foam or recycled packaging foam. I use all fiber for my pieces, but I'll show you how to use fillers as a shortcut without sacrificing the awesome felty end product.

## FUNCTIONAL FILLERS

You can use marbles, rocks, pipe cleaners and more to turn your creations into functional art pieces or just to give them some weight. Inserts can help you stabilize a little felt friend or help give it bendy arms to wrap around you.

## SEWING NOTIONS AND JEWELRY FINDINGS

Felt is a fabric, even if it's sculpted into a 3D form. Use all the traditional sewing goodies and jewelry findings to add flair or functionality to your projects.

## OTHER FABRIC

You can needle felt onto fabrics of all kinds, including fleece and commercial-made felt, which comes in different thicknesses and lots of cool colors.

## BROKEN THINGS

You can upcycle bits of shiny garbage and busted toys by embedding or attaching them to your felted projects. I love the unexpected things you can create, and the personal touches you can add when using stuff you never thought could be fixed but couldn't bear giving up. Now you have a really cool reason to use all those pieces you've been collecting over the years.

*You can always start a project with a thicker fiber like Corriedale and then add a few final layers of finer fiber or blends to give your project a special finish.*

### Save Everything

*There's no end to the fun you can have with the little stray fiber tumbleweeds that end up on your table, floor or shirt. Keep rejected felted pieces and any edges you may have cut off. If nothing else, these are great to put inside larger sculptures or to use as stuffing for toys.*

# TECHNIQUES

I invite you to treat these basic techniques as exercises. If you take a little time to make some flat fabric, a ball, a disc and a log without the fear or worries that can get inside your head when you start a major project, you will have more understanding of the fundamentals of felting than you can imagine. These practice parts can be the seeds that help your future projects grow.

## The Biggest Tip of All

The solution to a lot of felting challenges is to add more fiber, so build your pieces slowly, layer by layer, so you always have the option to add more if needed. Soft and squishy? Add more fiber. Unsightly bumpy surface? Add more fiber. Still too small? Add more fiber. Use small wisps and lots of gentle poking until you like what you've made.

## "Am I done yet?"

The answer is more flexible than you think. You get to decide how you want your finished piece to look and feel, but first it's all about function. For instance, if you're making something for heavy-duty/everyday use, you want to make sure the piece is strong with all attachments or seams made extra secure. If you're making something more decorative, or a plushy to squeeze, you can afford to leave the finished piece a little fuzzy and soft. So ask yourself, "If I stop now, is my piece structurally sound? Will it do the job I want it to do?" When the answer is "yes" then any further attention to detail is up to you and your personal felting style. You are the artist, so you get to choose.

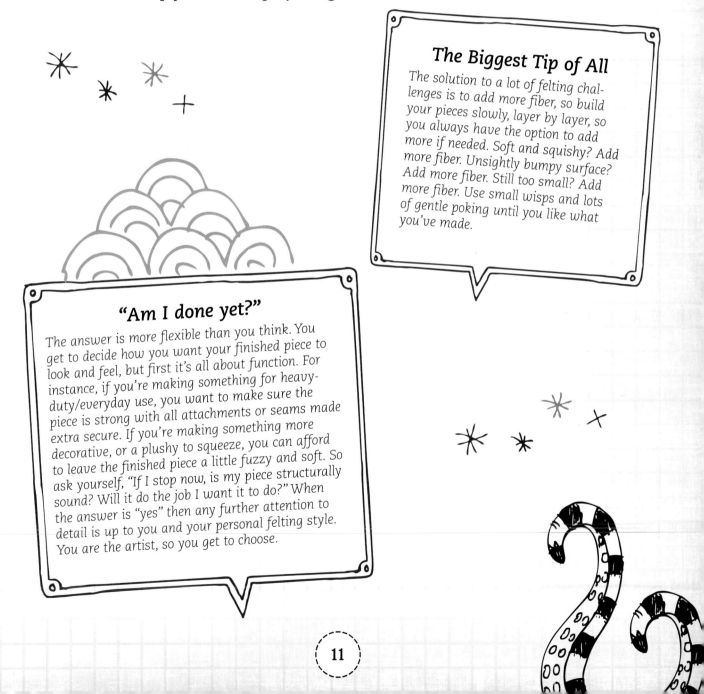

# DEPTH OF POKES

Let's get friendly with the most important companions in your felting adventures: needles.

## Materials & Tools

multi-needle
felting tool

single felting
needles

### Note

*Even when you poke all the way to the pink area on the needle, it doesn't, and shouldn't, mean using a lot of force. Gentle pokes for all needle depths are not only safer for your fingers, but are also far more effective for your felting. It's win-win!*

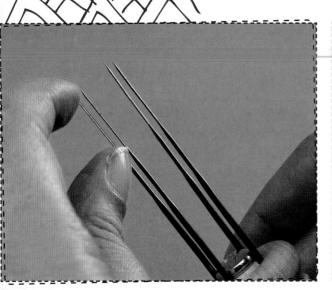

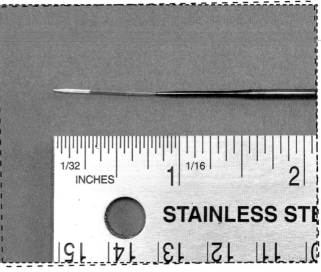

### Needles

The sharp, pointy section I'm showing between my fingers is the business end of the felting needle. Any higher up than my thumb and the needle has no more notches. Poking any further than that just wastes your energy. The needles pictured above are part of a multi-needle felting tool.

### Needle Depth of Poke

I painted this single needle to make it easier to understand the different kinds of poking. When you start felting things, the levels and effectiveness of each level will become a more organic part of the process. This painted needle is only for reference; a painted needle is a retired needle.

The very tip (painted white) is what we use for tiny or shallow pokes. This is good for delicate detailing and for smoothing surfaces, edges and seams.

Poke all the way through the yellow section when building mass in your 3D projects.

The pink section is the limit, used for making fabric or very large, thick sculptures.

## 1. Pull some fiber

Gently pull the fiber apart into tufts, approximately 2½" × 2½" (6.5cm × 6.5cm).

## 2. Lay out the first layer of fiber

Spread the tufts with your fingers to keep them thin and even. Lay the tufts in a row on your foam, all going in the same direction and overlapping each other about ½" (1.5cm). Continue to lay tufts in rows, each row slightly overlapping the last.

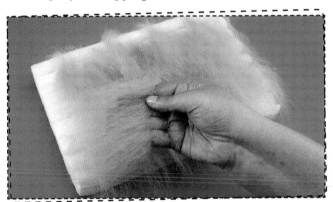

## 3. Lay out the second layer

Repeat steps 1 and 2, but this time lay out the rows perpendicular to the first layer, keeping the tufts about the same size, evenly spaced and overlapping each other.

# CREATING FLAT FABRIC

Essentially, you're making a homemade version of the commercial felt you find in craft stores. This technique allows you to create with your favorite colors and fibers.

## Materials & Tools

1 oz. wool fiber
in desired color

foam

1 multi-needle
felting tool

1 single felting needle

### Note

*What you want to make with your felt dictates how much of the foam you need to cover. You can lay out an area specific to the size of your final project or cover the whole foam and cut the pieces to size when you've finished felting it. (If you do cut your felt to size, you'll need to add a bit of fiber to the cut edges to finish them smoothly.)*

**Tip**

*The fiber pulls more easily if you place your hands about 4"–5" (10cm–12.5cm) apart and pull gently from the end. Using scissors to cut the fibers, especially at this point, isn't a good idea. Cut fibers don't felt easily.*

## 4. Build up fiber layers

Repeat steps 1–3 so there are a total of 4 layers of fiber, each perpendicular to the one before. Make sure the fiber is laid out as evenly as possible.

## 5. Felters, start your poking

Punch the felting tool into the fibers in firm but shallow punches. Make sure the tool stays at a 90-degree angle to the foam; this will help keep the fiber in place and the needles safe from breaking.

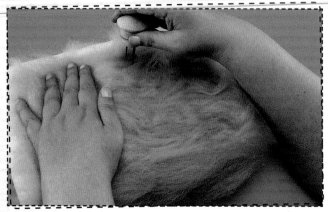

## 6. Keep poking the fiber

Continue punching the tool across the surface of the wool until it begins to flatten. If you feel like it's not working, try a little more pressure. Guess what? You're felting!

## 7. Flip flattened fiber

When the wool starts to flatten and come together, gently scrunch it, pull it off of the foam and flip it over. Continue to felt on the other side. You don't have to concentrate on every inch of fiber. Instead, poke the tool into the fiber in multiple spots and flip it over again.

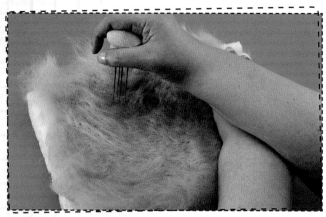

## 8. Keep on poking

Flip the fiber often and felt this way on both sides. This makes the fibers lock more quickly and helps the longevity of the foam.

**Tip**

*A little flaking foam is normal, as is a little fiber embedding in the foam. However, if your foam is coming off into the felt in big chunks, you're not flipping enough. And if you find a whole lot of fiber embedding in your foam, you may be punching too hard.*

### Angled Poking

*Once you get to step 8 or so, you can change the angle of your poking as needed, but be sure to poke in and out at the same angle. Don't change direction mid-poke or you'll probably break some needles off in the foam. Why poke at an angle? Sometimes you can further condense and shrink your felt piece by poking toward the center instead of straight up and down.*

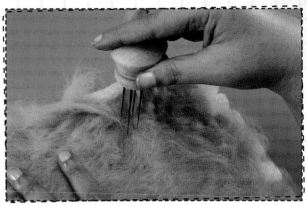

### 9. Bring in the edges

Fold the thinnest fuzzy part of the edges towards the center and poke them down to incorporate them into the fabric.

### 11. Cover up thin spots

To fix the weak areas, add a thin wisp of felt over the spot. Add another thin wisp of the same size and lay it perpendicular.

### 10. Check for thin spots

Hold the felt up to the light to detect any uneven or weak areas where light shows through.

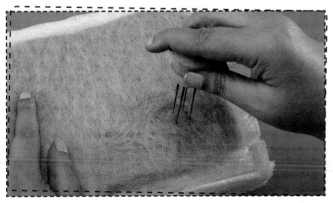

### 12. Poke it some more

Continue poking and flipping, incorporating the cover-up fiber and continuing to condense the rest of the felt.

### 13. All poked out?

Repeat steps 10–12 until you're satisfied with the look and texture of the flat fabric.

## Finishing Flat Fabric

Let's pretend you're making a wallet. You're done with all your embellishing and detail work and you're ready to finish it off. You can sew it closed, or use a decorative embroidery closing stitch. The cool part is that you can also felt it closed, and here's how.

### 1. Line up the edges

Create a piece of flat fabric (see Creating Flat Fabric on page 13). Fold the flat fabric into the desired finished shape.

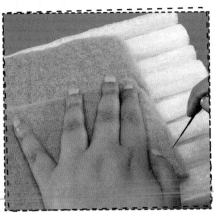

### 2. Poke the sides

Place the folded fabric on the foam. Use a single needle to poke the edges together.

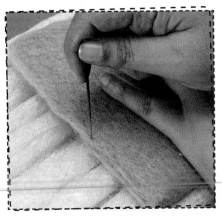

### 3. Poke the sides some more

Flip the folded fabric over and felt the edges some more. Repeat this several times until the seams start to adhere.

### 4. Hide the seams

Use tiny pokes on the seams from the outside in to further secure the seams and to make a smooth finish.

### 5. Extra help

If needed, you can place a small piece of foam inside the folded fabric to help keep it stable.

### 6. Add fiber

You may want to add some little wisps of fiber to the edges, especially if you had to cut the flat fabric to size. This helps make the edges look nice and gives a strong bond to the seams.

**Tip**

*Avoid scissors when you can. Cutting fiber makes the ends angry and sharp; angry and sharp fibers don't play well with others and, thus, don't felt together easily. If you make a boo-boo and felt something together by mistake, pulling the fibers apart, instead of cutting, is ideal.*

# 3D PART 1: SHAPES

Needle felting in 3D is like sculpting with wool instead of clay. As many shapes as there are in the universe, so are the number of shapes you can needle felt. But first, here are some useful fundamental shapes to play with.

## Felt a Ball

This simple shape can be the basis for your tabletop bowling set or a dolly's head. Learn how to make a lovely round sphere, then celebrate!

### 1. Pull some fiber

Gently pull a tuft of fiber (about 3" [7.5cm] long). Pinch and pull the fiber apart a few times to loosen and tangle them a bit. If you want a marbled look, use several colors and mix them together during the pinching and pulling process (see Color Blending on page 35).

### 2. Roll the fiber

Roll the fiber wad into a not-at-all precise but relatively compact ball.

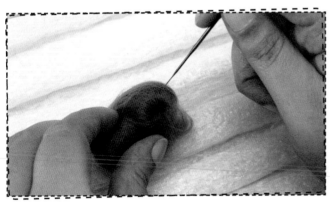

### 3. Start poking

Lay the fiber wad on the foam and gently poke it from all sides with a single felting needle. Remember to lift and move the ball often so you don't permanently attach it to the foam.

### 4. Keep poking

Continue to gently poke the ball from all sides, and move it around the foam. The more you poke, the smaller and denser the ball will become.

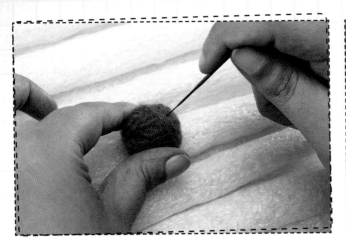

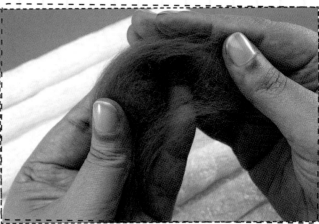

### 5. More tiny pokes

As the ball gets dense, use tiny pokes to shape and smooth the surface (See Needle Depth of Poke on page 12).

### 6. Add fiber

If you reach the desired size but the ball isn't as thick or as strong as you want it to be, pull a little more fiber, loosely wrap it around the ball and continue poking. If you want the ball to get bigger, you can add a thicker tuft of fiber.

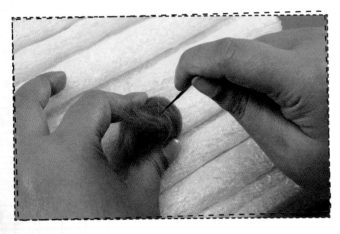

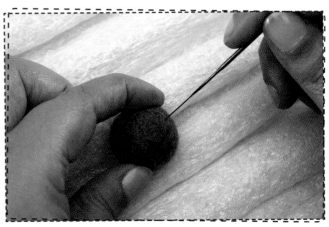

### 7. Keep going

Repeat this process as many times as it takes to get the ball to a size and texture that you love.

### 8. Tiny pokes for the win

Use tiny pokes all over the surface to smooth and finish the ball.

**Tip** *Even if the ball is to size and is strong enough, using very tiny pokes to add a thin wispy final layer of fiber will smooth out the surface even more.*

## Felt a Puck

Pucks have a versatile shape and can be morphed into felt cookies, ashtrays, yo-yos and more. The puck's width and overall shape are up to you, but this basic technique will help you achieve those dreams.

## Materials & Tools

wool fiber in color of your choice

foam

1 single felting needle

### 1. Pull some fiber

Gently pull a tuft of fiber (about 3" [7.5cm] long).

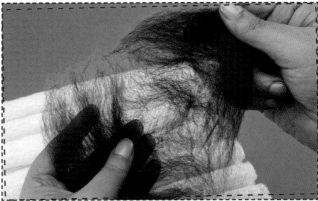

### 2. Tangle the fiber

Loosen the tuft a bit, pulling the sides to tangle the fiber and make it wispy. Pinch and pull the tuft to further tangle the fibers.

### 3. Form fiber shape

Fold the fiber into a not-at-all perfect puffy disc, about 2½" (6.5cm) in diameter.

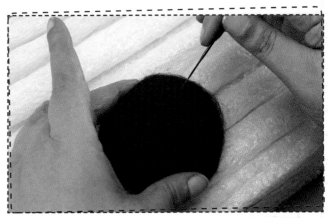

### 4. Start poking

Using a single needle, gently poke the disc from the top. As soon as it begins to hold its shape, flip it over and poke the other side.

**Tip** *Just as with creating flat felt, make sure your pokes go in and out in the same direction. Don't change direction mid-poke or you'll probably break your needle off in the foam or in your piece.*

## 5. Begin to poke the edge

After the disc has some thickness, hold it on its side and use very gentle, shallow pokes to shape and flatten the edges (see Needle Depth of Poke on page 12).

## 6. Work the edge

Roll the disc and delicately poke the edges all the way around.

## 7. Add fiber

If you reach your desired size but the disc isn't as thick or as strong as you want it to be, pull a little more fiber, loosely wrap it around the disc and keep poking. If you want the disc to get bigger, you can add a thicker tuft of fiber.

## 8. Keep going

After adding the fiber, repeat step 4, poking the disc top and bottom.

## 9. And going

Keep refining the edge of the disc as you did at step 6.

## 10. Aaaaaand going

Work the edge of the disc, using tiny shallow pokes to make it flat and clean. Repeat steps 7–10 as many times as needed to finish the disc to your liking.

## Felt a Log

Turn it into an arm, a giraffe neck, or trunk or just leave it as a log, log, log!

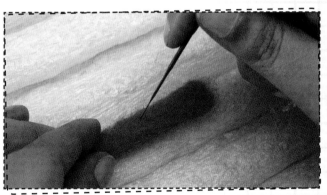

Materials & Tools

wool fiber in color
of your choice

foam

1 single felting needle

### 1. Pull some fiber

Gently pull a tuft of fiber (about 2" [5cm] long). Pinch and pull the fiber apart a few times to loosen and tangle the fibers a bit.

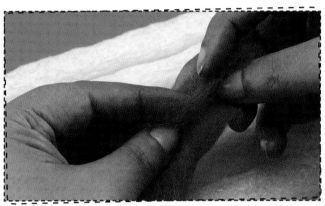

### 2. Form a log

Fold the fiber into a not-at-all perfect puffy log shape.

### 3. Poke the log

Place the fiber on the foam. Using gentle pokes with a single needle, begin to felt the log.

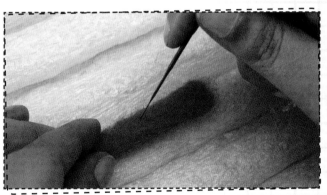

### 4. Poke and move

Continue poking the log from all angles, making sure to move it around the foam so it doesn't get stuck.

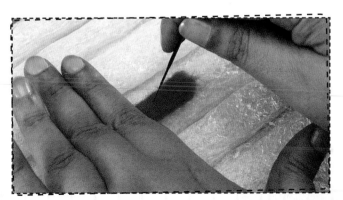

### 5. Roll the log

Continue poking the log, rolling it along the foam as you go to keep it uniform.

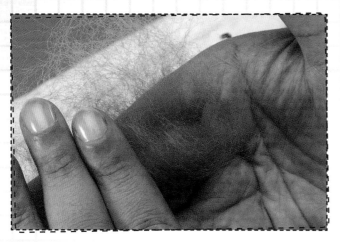

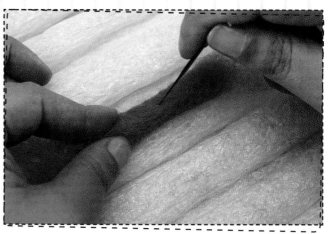

## 6. Add fiber

If you reach your desired size but the log isn't as thick or as strong as you want it to be, pull a little more fiber, loosely wrap it around the log and keep poking. If you want the log to get bigger, you can add a thicker tuft of fiber.

## 7. Keep poking and rolling

Continue poking the log from all angles, making sure to move it around the foam so it doesn't get stuck.

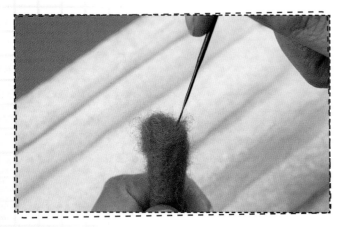

## 8. Poke ends

When the log is as thick and round as you want it, stand it on one end and gently poke the fuzzy end down to flatten it.

## 9. Work ends

Use tiny, shallow pokes straight into the end to make the edge flat and smooth (See Needle Depth of Poke on page 12). If you want it to be rounded on the end, add a tiny wisp of fiber to the tip and use gentler pokes to keep it rounded. Repeat steps 6–9 as many times as needed to finish the log to your liking. Finish both ends, or leave one fuzzy if you want to attach the log to another piece (see Forming Attachments on page 23).

# 3D PART II: FORMING ATTACHMENTS

It's much easier to connect several finished pieces of 3D felt to each other than it is to make a complicated sculpture all at once. If you are making an octopus, for example, you probably want to felt the body and each tentacle separately, attaching them together at the end. But for the sake of this example, let's pretend that what you really want to make is a ball with a log on it. C'mon, everybody loves a ball with a log on it!

## Materials & Tools

wool fiber in colors
of your choice

foam

1 single felting needle

## A Word on Fuzzy Edges

*If you don't have any fuzzy, it's much harder to attach pieces or seams. It's often helpful to leave the end of your piece on the fuzzy side if you know that you want to connect it to another piece. If you fully felted something, or had to cut it, and decide later that you want to attach it, you'll want to take a wisp of fiber and poke it into the connection spot.*

### 1. It takes two

Make a ball and a log. This time, only poke the log flat on one end. The fuzzy end is the glue that will help get these two crazy kids together. (See Felt a Ball on page 17 and Felt a Log on page 21.)

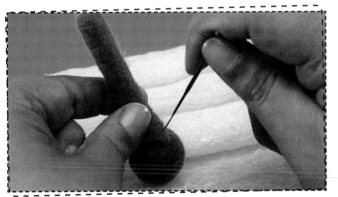

### 2. Secure the log to the ball

Hold the fuzzy end of the log onto the ball wherever you want it to live. Gently poke the fibers from the bottom of the log into the ball to anchor the log into place.

### 3. Keep poking the fuzzy

Continue to poke the fuzzy part of the log into the ball, turning it as you go so you poke the fiber all around the log base.

## 4. Add fiber

If you feel like the connection isn't secure enough, add a tiny strip of fiber around the base of the log.

## 5. Poke in new fiber

Incorporate the new fiber wisp by poking diagonally into the log and the ball, further securing them together.

## 6. Clean up

Repeat steps 4–5 if needed. Use gentle pokes around the edge of the log to clean up any stray fuzzy bits. (May the ball and log live together happily for the rest of their days.)

### A World of Possibilities

Now the rest of the shapes in the universe are at your fingertips. By felting shapes and combining them, you can make whatever you heart desires. Visualizing the shape of what you want to create is the key to 3D felting, but don't feel like you have to work without a net. If you want to felt an owl, for example, you'll have an easier time achieving shapes and proportions if you can see the real deal as you go. Unless you keep an owl as a pet, it can be handy to use a photo, drawing or even a template as a reference.

# 3D PART III: EMBEDDING OBJECTS

If you want a felted piece to bend, you might felt around a wire armature. If you want to make something large but don't want to felt it from scratch, you can felt around Styrofoam or other foam balls, cones or cubes. You can incorporate other objects, too. Felt around a boulder to block your office door from the inside. A film canister with some popcorn kernels inside can be the base of a noise-making toy to irritate babies. Felt around some soap and you've got sudsy and exfoliating felty fun. Whatever your reasons, it's easy to snuggle objects inside your felted creations.

## Making an Armature

When you felt around wires, it feels kind of crunchy against the needle. Use very deliberate, gentle pokes so the needle can slide itself next to the wires when it makes contact. You should also know that felting around wire or other objects will definitely dull your needles more quickly than plain old felting. These instructions can be used for pipe cleaners and wire.

## Materials & Tools

wool fiber

foam

1 multi-needle felting tool

1 single felting needle

pipe cleaners or craft wire

Note: The thicker the final felted piece will be, the thicker and stronger the wire needs to be in order to bend and keep its shape under the felt.

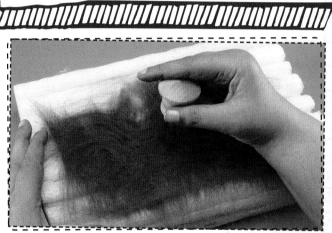

### 1. Make thin, flat fabric

Follow the flat felting instructions but use only 2 layers of fiber (see Creating Flat Fabric on page 13). Leave the flat fabric on the foam when you are finished with this step.

### 2. Prepare underwire

Take two pieces of pipe cleaner, or fold one pipe cleaner in half, leaving a small loop at the top, and twist the ends together. Pull the pipe cleaner apart in some spots to make a few gaps.

### 3. Make fiber anchors

Pull a few thin wisps of fiber through a few of the gaps in the pipe cleaners. This provides anchor spots for the wrapped fiber to grab onto.

25

## 4. Tuck and roll

Place the armature on the thin flat fabric at the edge closest to you. Holding the edge of the fabric, roll the armature and fabric edge away from you, keeping the armature tucked tightly inside the fabric.

## 5. Poke it into place

Use a single needle to poke along the outside of the tucked fabric edge, securing the armature in the cocoon.

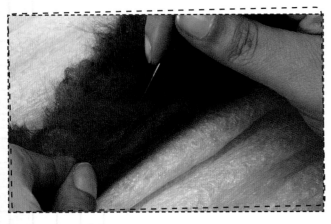

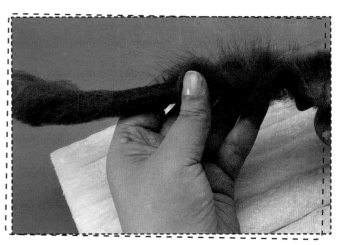

## 6. Keep tucking and rolling

Roll the now-snuggly armature away from you and poke the edge at each turn, tightly securing the armature inside.

## 7. Add fiber

Pull a little more fiber, loosely wrap it around the armature log and gently poke it all over.

## 8. Ta da!

Repeat steps 6 and 7 until you're satisfied with the size and feel of the piece and it bends to your every whim.

## Soft Objects

If you want to use a non-traditional shape as a base, you can carve whatever shape you like from thick pieces of polystyrene or upholstery foam. Given a choice, I'll pick spongy soft foam instead of Styrofoam for embedding, no matter what shape is needed.

### Materials & Tools

```
wool fiber
foam
1 multi-needle felting tool
1 single felting needle
foam ball
```

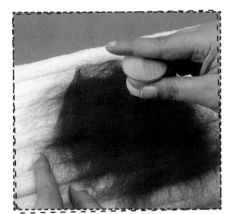

### 1. Make thin, flat fabric

Follow the flat felting instructions but use only 2 layers of fiber (see Creating Flat Fabric on page 13).

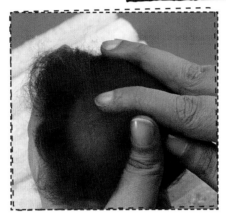

### 2. Wrap it up

Hold the foam ball and wrap the thin fabric around it. It's OK if the flat fabric is uneven or if it overlaps.

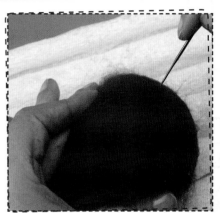

### 3. Secure the ball

Hold the fabric around the ball and gently poke it into place. It's not important for the needle to penetrate the ball deeply.

### 4. Keep poking

Rotate the fabric and ball and continue poking all over.

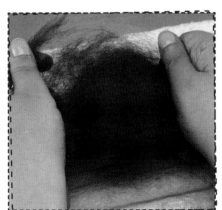

### 5. Thicken the skin

Pull apart a tuft of fiber to make it thin and wispy and lay it over the ball.

### 6. More poking

Repeat steps 4–5 as needed to cover any thin spots, to build bulk and to grow the ball to the desired size and texture.

## Hard Objects

Embedding a soft object can save you some time, but embedding a hard object can add function. You can hide magnets, clips, washers and more to turn your felt creations into playable and wearable pieces.

```
Materials & Tools
wool fiber
foam
1 multi-needle felting tool
1 single felting needle
1 large marble
```

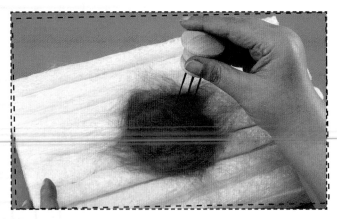

### 1. Make thin, flat fabric

Follow the flat felting instructions but use only 2 layers of fiber (see Creating Flat Fabric on page 13).

### 2. Wrap up the marble

Wrap the fabric around the marble and hold it in place. It's OK if the flat fabric is uneven or if it overlaps.

### 3. Poke, but with great care

Use diagonal pokes to felt the flat fabric around the marble. Because you can't poke directly into a marble or other hard object, your pokes need to be diagonal and require extreme caution. Instead of felting straight into a fiber mass, you are felting a skin around the marble; diagonal pokes tighten that skin.

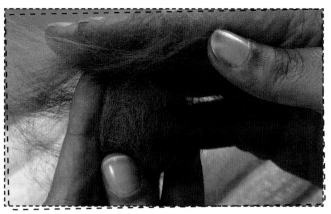

### 4. Add fiber

As soon as the fabric is holding on to the marble, wrap a loose wisp of fiber around it and continue your diagonal pokes. Repeat steps 3–4 as needed to thicken the skin, build bulk and to grow the ball to the desired size and texture.

# EMBELLISHING

Decoration is where you can let your imagination run loose like a crazy weasel. After you've made something out of felt, it can be embellished like any other fabric: try sewing, embroidery, buttons, ribbons, appliqué, zippers, sequins, findings, snaps, etc. Of course, you can add lots of details with more needle felting, too. Use the following techniques to embellish any of your felted creations, flat or 3D.

## Materials & Tools

wool fiber for accent

foam

1 multi-needle felting tool

1 single felting needle

## Make a Stripe, Straight Up

I heard a rumor once that some people who want to draw or felt or paint a straight line use a ruler as a guide. I suppose this would work just fine, but being the impatient non-prep person I am, I prefer to do it without a map. If you are a ruler person, I salute you … rule away!

### 1. Pull some fiber

For the purposes of this exercise, create a piece of flat fabric (see Creating Flat Fabric on page 13).

Gently pull a small thin tuft of fiber from your accent fiber (about 1" [2.5cm] long).

### 2. Make the fiber thinner

Pull the accent fiber at the ends to thin it out.

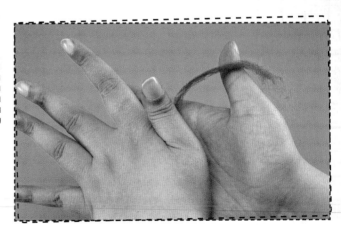

### 3. Palm it

Roll the accent fiber to create a loose rope.

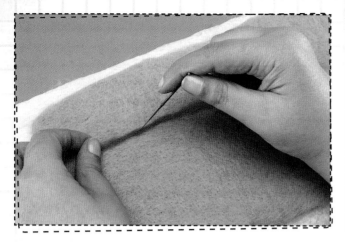

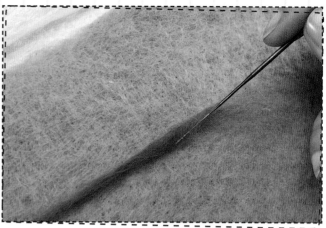

## 4. Poke the center

Lay the accent fiber on the flat fabric (or the surface of your 3D object). Slowly and carefully poke the center of the accent fiber with the single needle to anchor it into place. (If you have a wide stripe, you can use a multi-needle tool to make quick work of this step.)

## 5. Poke the edges

Use the single needle to poke the edges of the accent stripe into place. By twisting the fuzzy edges of the accent fiber around the needle tip and poking towards the center of the stripe, you make the stripe thicker and straighter at the same time. Refining and poking the edges wherever there are stray fibers make the line clean and defined.

Continue to poke the accent line all over to secure it. Add more thin wisps of fiber to the ends of the stripe as needed for length or thickness.

### Watch Your Back

Keep in mind while you plan the overall design of your piece that the accent color will start to come through the back of the felt.

## Make a Stripe, Mix It Up

Your accents can be as interesting and shapely as you want them to be; make it swirly, wavy, boxy, bouncy or a zigzag like I made here. Lead the fiber around like a dog on a leash and poke it where you want it to stay.

## Materials & Tools

wool fiber for accent

foam

1 multi-needle felting tool

1 single felting needle

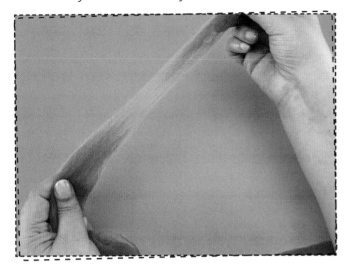

### 1. Pull some fiber

For the purposes of this exercise, create a piece of flat fabric (see Creating Flat Fabric on page 13).

Gently pull a long thin tuft of the accent fiber (about 1½" [4cm] long).

### 2. Palm it

Roll the accent fiber to create a loose rope.

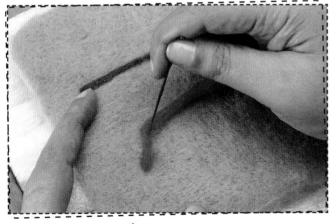

### 3. Arrange the stripe

Use a single needle to poke the end of the accent fiber into place. Hold the fiber where you want it to go and poke the next anchor spot to secure it to the fabric. Use more pokes along the fiber back to the starting point to felt it down.

### 4. Bring it down

Pull the accent fiber into place for the next zigzag and poke it loosely into place.

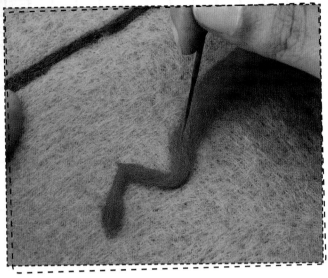

### 5. Up again

Pull the fiber into place for the next zigzag and poke it loosely into place.

### 6. Down it goes

Pull the fiber into place for the next zigzag and poke it loosely into place.

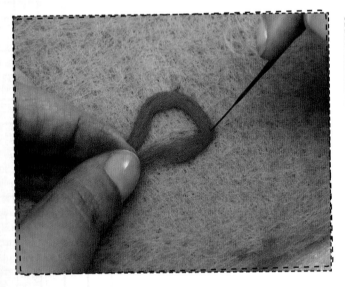

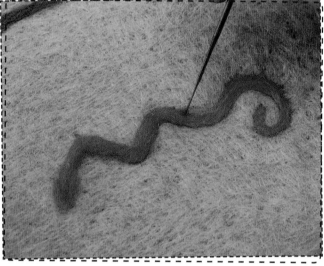

### 7. Round out your design

To finish this accent stripe, hold the fiber in place in a curve at the end, then poke it loosely into place.

### 8. Finish the embellishment

Go back over the stripe, poking thoroughly along the way to flatten it and tidy the edges. If needed, add thin wisps of fiber to fill out thin spots or to make the stripe longer.

## Poke-a-Dot, Flat and Fine

Fewer things are cuter than a polka-dot. I like my mine to have clearly defined edges, so steps 4 and 5 are very important to me. Feel free to be fuzzy, though ... you are the master of your own destiny.

## Materials & Tools

wool fiber for accent

foam

1 multi-needle felting tool

1 single felting needle

### 1. Pull some fiber

For the purposes of this exercise, create a piece of flat fabric (see Creating Flat Fabric on page 13).

Gently pull a small thin tuft of accent fiber (about ½" [1.5cm] long).

### 2. Shape the fiber

Fold the tuft to make a small loose disc.

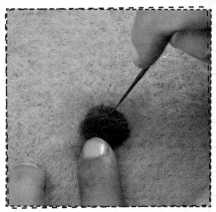

### 3. Secure the dot

Use a single needle to poke into the center of the loose disc to anchor it in place on the flat fabric (or the 3D object).

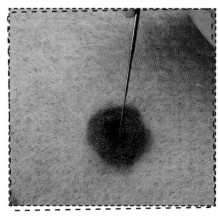

### 4. Keep poking

Straight up and down, continue poking the surface of the polka dot. At the fuzzy edge of the dot, gently twist the stray bits of fiber around the needle and poke them toward the center of the dot. By twisting, the fuzzy edges of the accent fiber around the needle tip and then poking toward the center of the dot, you make the edges clearly defined.

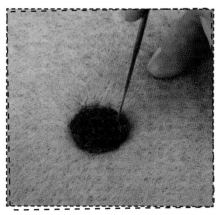

### 5. Poke around the edge

Keep poking around the edge of the polka dot, shaping and cleaning as you go.

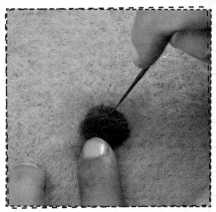

### 6. Add fiber

If necessary, lay another thin wisp of fiber on top of the polka dot and poke it into place to fill any thin spots.

Repeat steps 4–6 until you have a dot you love.

## Poke-a-Dot, Puffy Style

The key to a puffy dot is to use light shallow pokes to give the fiber dot a crispy shell coating while leaving the innards big and puffy.

```
Materials & Tools
wool fiber for accent
foam
1 multi-needle felting tool
1 single felting needle
```

### 1. Pull some fiber

For the purposes of this exercise, create a piece of flat fabric (see Creating Flat Fabric on page 13).

Gently pull a small thin tuft of accent fiber (about ½" [1.5cm] long).

### 2. Shape the fiber

Fold the tuft to make a small loose ball.

### 3. Secure the ball

Use a single needle to anchor the ball to the flat fabric (or onto a 3D surface) with a few gentle pokes in the center.

### 4. Poke the edge

Gently poke and tuck the edge underneath and toward the center of the ball and into the flat fabric. This will help secure the dot, making it puffy instead of flat, like a bouffant hairdo.

### 5. Add fiber

If necessary, lay another thin wisp of fiber on top of the puffy dot and poke it all the way around the edge to secure it.

### 6. Poke the surface

Use very shallow gentle pokes over the top of the ball to create a softly felted surface without flattening the shape. Repeat step 4 if necessary, making sure the dot is securely fastened to the felt.

# COLOR BLENDING

You can use pre-mixed fiber batts, or lay accent colors on top of your almost-finished project to give it a spontaneous-looking color blend. Here's a simple way to mix up some fiber colors of your own—customize as you desire.

## Materials & Tools

wool fiber (at least two colors)

### 1. Pull some fiber from first color

Gently pull a tuft of fiber (about 2" [5cm] long).

### 2. Pull some fiber from second color

Gently pull a tuft of the same size of your second fiber color.

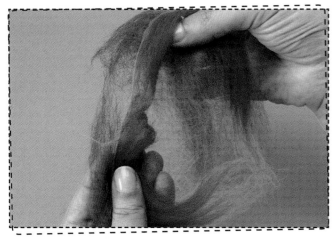

### 3. Pull them apart

Holding both colors, pull at the edges of the fiber, loosening them and making them wispy.

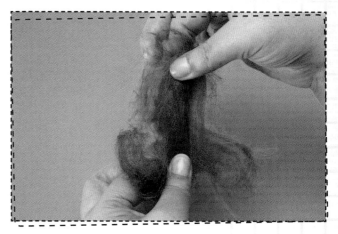

### 4. Twist and pull

Pinch and pull the fibers apart and bring them back together, mixing the colors until you're satisfied with the blend.

After you mix it up, you can use the new fiber blend just like any other fiber.

# WEARABLES

A lot of the projects in this section are thematic twists on conventional accessories; I like to play with traditional styles and contradictions. I do love the elegance of my grandmother's pearls, but I'm likely to wear them with combat boots. Wearing art pieces like these can be a lot more fun than your average jewelry; not just because you made them yourself, but because they often start interesting conversations.

LLO
NAME IS
efty

# MARTINI-TIME NECKLACE

This necklace was inspired by the sophisticated grace of knotted pearls and the juicy deliciousness of the gourmet martini olive.

## Materials & Tools

wool fiber in green and red

foam

1 single felting needle

translucent beading floss

sewing needle

elegant clasp

scissors

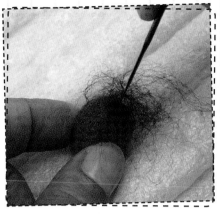

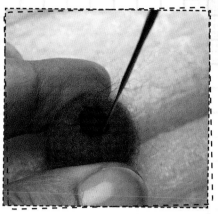

### 1. Make an olive base

Loosely roll a tuft of green fiber into a quarter-sized ball with your fingertips (see Felt a Ball on page 17). As the fibers begin to pull together, form the olive shape by gently pushing on one end of the ball while poking the middle. Poke the ends to keep them rounded and to stop your olive from becoming too cylindrical.

### 2. Add a pimiento

When you've gotten the desired shape and size, take a wisp of red fiber and create a loose ball about the size of a baby pea. Hold the ball to the end of the olive and carefully poke through the red into the green. Use small pokes with the tip of the needle to twist and secure the edges of the red fiber into the olive.

### 3. Tuck in the pimiento

As you embed the pimiento, also poke the green area around it, creating the "pitted" area of the olive. Add more red fiber if you want a bigger pimiento; add green if your olive needs more size, shape or thickness.

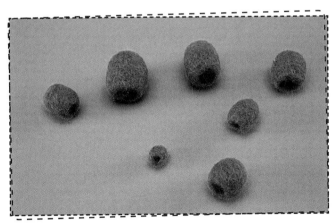

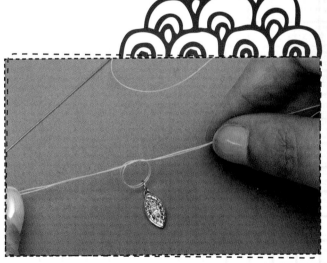

### 4. Make more olives

Repeat steps 1–3 to make 7–10 olives in a variety of sizes, all smaller than a real olive to give the necklace a delicate quality.

### 5. Start the necklace

Thread the sewing needle with the beading floss and pull the ends together, creating a double strand. Attach one part of the clasp to the loose end of the floss using whatever method your clasp dictates. This one just ties to the end with several knots.

## 6. Add an olive

Push the needle through an olive at whatever angle makes you happy.

## 7. Knot it

Pull the olive down until it rests on the clasp. Make an overhand knot as close to the olive as possible. Gently pull the two threads apart to slide the knot snugly against the olive as it tightens.

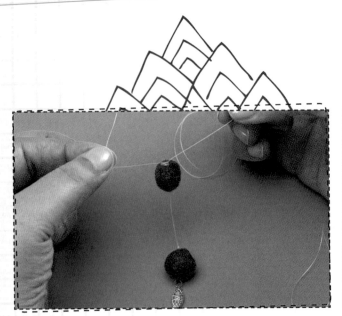

## 8. Keep stringing and knotting

Make another knot about 1" (2.5cm) down the floss. String an olive and secure it like you did the last one. Continue to knot and string olives until you reach your desired necklace length.

## 9. Finish up

Attach the second half of the clasp to the needle end of the floss. Trim the excess floss with the scissors and get thee to a cocktail party.

# CUFFED (AKA PROJECTILE GROMMETING)

The thickness and width of the felt combined with the hardware feel of the grommets make this a capital "C" Cuff. The soft merino wool, watercolor-ish transitions and delicate silver findings kick it over into the jewelry category. So wear it to the opera, grocery store, or a tractor pull ... you'll fit in anywhere you go.

## Materials & Tools

wool fiber in blue and lavender

foam

1 multi-needle felting tool

1 single felting needle

scissors

2 ½" (1.5cm) grommets

1 ⅜" (1cm) grommet

grommet tool

hammer

2 silver bubble findings

translucent beading floss

sewing needle

silver clasp findings

needle-nose pliers

## 1. Lay out the first layer

Create a piece of fabric to fit the desired wrist, allowing at least ¼" (6mm) of fuzzy on each end like in Creating Flat Fabric on page 13. In order to get the two-color blend in this cuff, alternate colors with each tuft, as you lay the fiber in a row on your foam. The tufts should be going in the same directions and overlapping each other.

## 2. Lay out the second layer

Repeat the process in step 1, but this time lay out the row perpendicular to the first layer, keeping each tuft about the same size and evenly spaced. The alternating colors on each layer won't match up precisely, but that's how you get the blended look between each color.

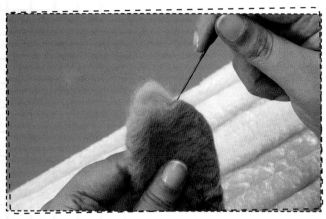

## 3. Finish the cuff base

After you've finished making the flat fabric, use tiny pokes with a single needle to shape and finish both cuff ends, poking down the fuzzy ends to match the shape of the bubble findings.

## 4. Prepare for the center grommet

Cut a small hole in the middle of the cuff, slightly smaller than the grommet. (If your grommets came with instructions, do what they tell ya!)

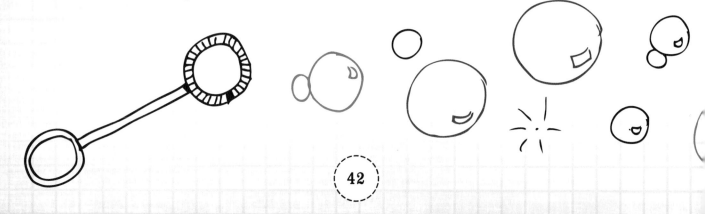

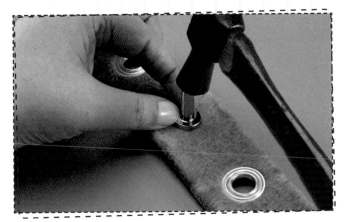

## 5. Install the grommet

Use the grommet tool and hammer to install the grommets according to the manufacturer's instructions. The small grommet should be placed in the center with big grommets on either side of the small one.

## 6. Fancy up the ends

Thread the sewing needle with the beading floss and sew a bubble finding to one end in several places to secure it to the fabric. Repeat on the other end of the fabric.

## 7. Hook it up

Use the needle-nose pliers to connect the clasp hook to the tip of one of the bubble findings.

## 8. Clasp for wear

To close the cuff, link the clasp hook through the tip of the bubble finding on the other end of the cuff and wear with joy.

# SPIKE ME

When you wear this hard-core spiked bracelet in the traditional punk-rock style, you can pretend to be a real tough customer ... but we all know you're really a softy.

## Materials & Tools

wool fiber in black and grey

foam

1 multi-needle felting tool

1 single felting needle

scissors

magnetic snap clasp

washer

needle-nose pliers

template for spike

## 1. Make the cuff base

Create a piece of fabric about ¼" (6mm) thick (the fabric in the flat fabric section is more like ⅛" [3mm]) to simulate leather, leaving at least 1" (2.5cm) fuzzy at both ends (see Creating Flat Fabric on page 13).

About 2" (5cm) down from one end, cut two small slits for the prongs of the snaps. Cut the slits so the prongs will be snug when inserted, or follow the snap manufacturer's instructions if they are provided.

## 2. Insert the snap

Push the prongs of the snap piece through the holes you made.

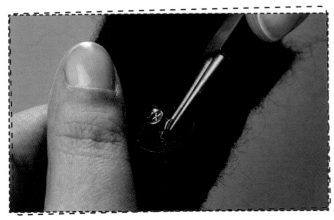

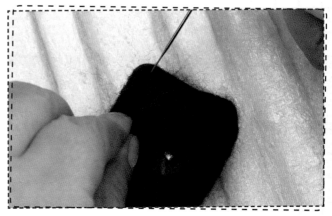

## 3. Secure the snap

Add the washer to the other side and use needle-nose pliers to bend the prongs around it.

## 4. Hide the snap

Fold the fuzzy end of the cuff over the washer side and poke it into place with the single needle, adding fiber if necessary to secure and cover up the washer.

## 5. Install the second snap

Repeat steps 1–4 to add the second half of the snap to the other side of the cuff, lining it up with the first half.

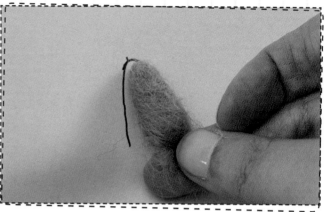

## 6. Make some spikes

Make spikes separately, leaving the larger end of the spike fuzzy (see 3D Part I: Shapes on page 17). Use the template to help keep each spike consistent, or mix it up by making a variety of sizes.

## 7. Attach the spikes

When you have enough spikes, 9 or 10, use a single needle to attach them, evenly spaced, to the cuff (see Forming Attachments on page 23).

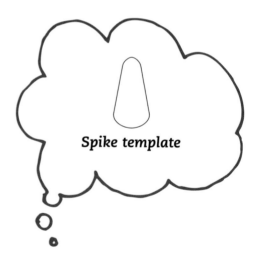

Spike template

# SOMEBODY SET UP US DA BOMB

A bomb pin is such a simple design, but with so many implications. It can represent your uncontainable spirit of rebellion. It might symbolize your rejection of court-mandated anger management classes. Maybe you're just a long-suffering coyote who, despite many disastrous results, can't stop buying things from the Acme Corporation. (If you make one in red, you'd be a "ch-ch-ch-ch-ch-ch-ch-ch-cherry bomb!!")

## Materials & Tools

wool fiber in black

foam

1 single felting needle

piece of white string

scissors

red marker

glue

pin back

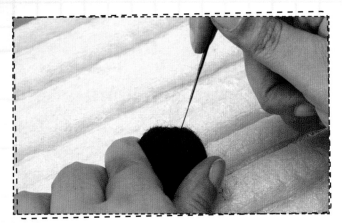

## 1. Make the bomb base

Using the single felting needle, make a ball about 1¼" (3cm) in diameter (see Felt a Ball on page 17). When the ball is close to your desired look, feel and size, decide where the back of your bomb will be. Poke the back of the ball to make a flatter surface for easy gluing.

## 2. Make the other part of da bomb

With a small tuft of black fiber, felt a short log shape for the wick base with one finished end and one fuzzy end (see Felt a Log on page 21). Attach the fuzzy end of the wick base to the top of the bomb (see Forming Attachments on page 23).

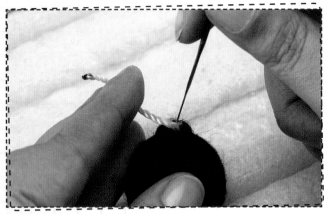

## 3. Install the fuse

Trim the white string to the desired size. Mark one end of the string with the red marker to make it sizzle. Use a single needle to attach the other end of the string into the top of the wick base.

## 4. Add the pin

Glue the pin to the flat side. Let the glue dry according to the glue manufacturer's instructions before wearing the pin.

# HAND CAMEO

When this brooch is pinned to your jacket, you will smile a little brighter, you'll stand a little taller and your eyes will twinkle with whimsy and mischief. How does the dolly feel about your brooch? She's probably not pleased, but she'll certainly think twice before she drinks all of the orange juice and puts the empty carton back in the refrigerator again.

## Materials & Tools

wool fiber in pink and white

foam

1 single felting needle

pin setting

glue

doll hand

scissors

HELLO
MY NAME IS
Lefty

49

## 1. Start the background

With the pink fiber, make an oval slightly larger than the framed area of the pin setting (see Felt a Puck on page 19).

## 2. Shape the background

Hold the disc in place in the pin setting and use gentle pokes to felt it into shape and size. Watch your fingers!

## 3. Secure the background

Glue the felt to the pin setting and allow it to dry.

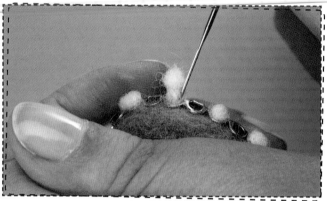

## 4. Make and attach the pearls

Use the white fiber to felt each individual "pearls," lightly felting a round shape with a fuzzy end (see Felt a Ball on page 17). Carefully felt the fuzzy end through the decorative loops on the pin setting into the pink oval.

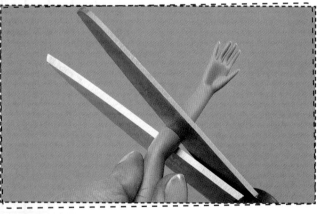

## 5. Get a hand

Snicker with evil glee or smile with gentle compassion as you separate the doll from her hand with scissors.

## 6. Attach the hand

Glue the doll hand to the center of the pink oval.

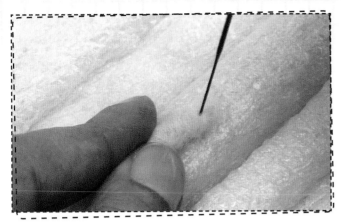

## 7. Make a doll bracelet base

Felt a tiny white bracelet with two fuzzy ends to fit around the doll wrist (see Felt a Log on page 21).

## 8. Detail the bracelet

Use pink fiber to add "jewels" to the doll bracelet (see Poke-a-Dot, Puffy Style on page 34).

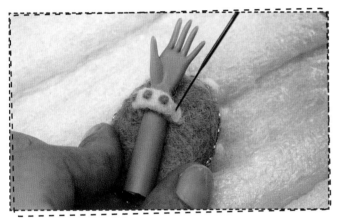

## 9. Attach the bracelet

When the glue on the hand is dry, poke the bracelet on each side of the doll wrist to attach it to the background.

## 10. Secure the bracelet

Use gentle pokes to tuck the bracelet ends underneath the doll wrist and into the background to further secure it into place.

# FAT HEAD

Felt can look funky-chunky and substantial while being lightweight enough to sit comfortably on your dainty skull. Why not embellish some extra-thick commercial felt with cutie-patootie details and stick it in your hairs?

## Materials & Tools

3mm or thicker commercial felt

scissors

wool fiber in orange, white and black

foam

1 single felting needle

embroidery thread

sewing needle

hair clip

## 1. Cut out a base

Cut the felt into a desired shape. You can trace a circle or rectangle, but free-form looks cooler in the end.

## 3. Grow your chick

Use thin wisps of orange fiber to make the triangle beak (see Embellishing on page 29). Use very thin wisps of the orange fiber to form the legs and feet.

## 5. Add edge details

Embellish the edge as desired. Here, I used a blanket stitch, but you can use felt, sew on beads, use a straight or other embroidery stitch, and so much more.

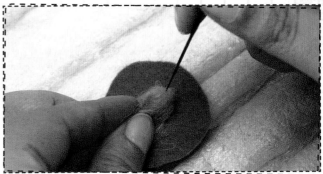

## 2. Make a chick body

Use a single needle to felt designs on the surface of the commercial felt. Make the body of the chick using the yellow fiber (see Poke-a-Dot, Puffy Style on page 34). Go gently because commercial felt this thick can be stubborn. You'll have to poke with more force and, therefore, more slowly.

## 4. Make an eye

Use a very small amount of black felt to make the eye. Roll the felt into a tiny ball and felt it into the chick body.

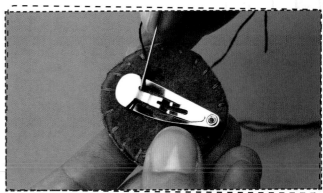

## 6. Add the hair clip

Use the sewing needle and embroidery thread to sew the clip to the back of the piece. Because the felt is so thick you don't have to sew through to the front.

# MEDIC ALERT BRACELET

Don't you hate it when you are getting ready to go to Thanksgiving dinner at your sister-in-law's house and you can feel your regular-as-clockwork holiday boredom, I mean, headache coming on? When you've got your medicine up your sleeve, you greatly improve your chances of feeling fantastic.

## Materials & Tools

wool fiber in cream, orange, red, yellow, green, pink and turquoise

foam

1 single felting needle

pill templates

black craft wire

wire cutters

round-nose pliers

needle-nose pliers

clasp findings

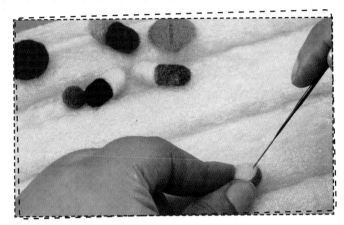

## 1. Make medicine, man

Make 7 or 8 pills in several shapes, sizes and colors (see 3D Part I: Shapes on page 17). Use the pill templates or "borrow" from the medicine cabinets of your loved ones and use them as reference material.

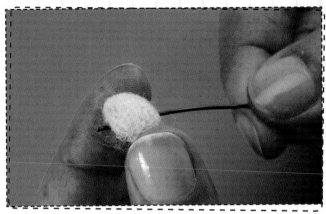

## 2. Stick a pill

Cut a piece of wire at an angle to create a pointy tip, at least twice the length of the first pill. Push the tip gently through the pill like you're making an Rx-kabob.

## 3. Make a loop

Use the round-nose pliers to make a loop on one end of the wire.

**Pill templates**

55

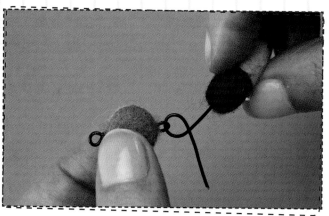

## 4. Wrap around

Grasp the loop with the round-nose pliers. Grasp the wire tail with the needle-nose pliers and wrap the end of the wire below the loop several times. Push the pill so it rests against the wrap you just made.

## 5. One pill after another

Make another wrapped loop at the open end of the wire so your first pill is secure with loops on each side. Repeat step 4–5 on a second pill, but, before wrapping the first loop, thread the new wire onto the loop of the first pill to create a chain of meds.

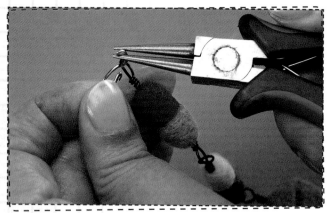

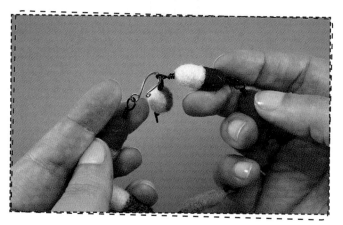

## 6. Chain-link drugs

Continue skewering the pills, looping and wrapping the wire and connecting each pill to the previous one. When you get to the end, add the clasp to one end.

## 7. Hook 'em

Hook the clasp through the second pill loop on the other end of the bracelet so the last bead dangles, and then rave on.

**Tip** *Beads are beads. After you've made your felted pills or felted beads of any kind, you can string them together with whatever beading method you love best.*

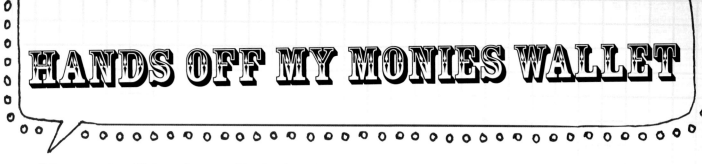

# HANDS OFF MY MONIES WALLET

"Guess what!? See that wallet? It's mine, right? Because we know it isn't yours, is it? Right. So, you see that lock on there? You know, the big lock on the wallet we already agreed is mine and not yours? Yeah, well that lock means you stay away from my monies, man. Understand? Do I need to explain it to you again or do you ... Hey! Where are you going?"

## Materials & Tools

wool fiber in magenta, green, black and grey

foam

1 multi-needle felting tool

1 single felting needle

lock and key templates

4 small round magnets

glue

## 1. Make the base

Using the magenta fiber, make a 9½" × 7" (24cm × 18cm) of flat fabric, medium thick, with finished top and bottom ends (see Creating Flat Fabric on page 13).

## 2. Lock and key

Using the templates, make the lock base with green and black fiber, and the lock U and the key with grey fiber (see 3D Part I: Shapes on page 17).

## 3. Fold for finesse

Fold the fabric so you can see how it will look when finished.

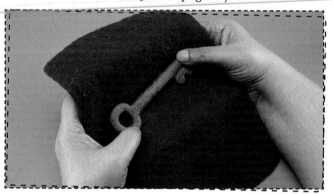

## 4. Fit the key first

Place the key on the back of the wallet and nudge it around until you like the placement. Hold it in place while you unfold the wallet.

## 5. Attach the key

Keep the key in place on the felt as you lay them both onto the foam. Gently poke the key around the edges into the felt to secure it into place (see Forming Attachments on page 23).

## 6. Lock in that lock

Flip over the fabric and poke into the back of the key to attach it even more. Be careful not to poke too deeply or the magenta will show through the front side of the key. Repeat this process for the lock base and U, laying them in place on the fabric, poking around the edges and flipping the fabric over to felt them from the other side.

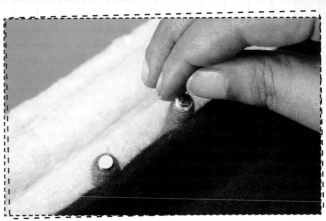

## 7. Finishing touches

Fold the fabric again and use a single needle or two to close the seams on each side of the wallet (see Finishing Flat Fabric on page 16). Make sure the lock top and bottom line up nicely.

## 8. Closure

Glue the magnets into place. Glue each magnet correctly so they attract instead of repel. Let the glue dry, stuff the wallet with monies and go buy yourself something nice.

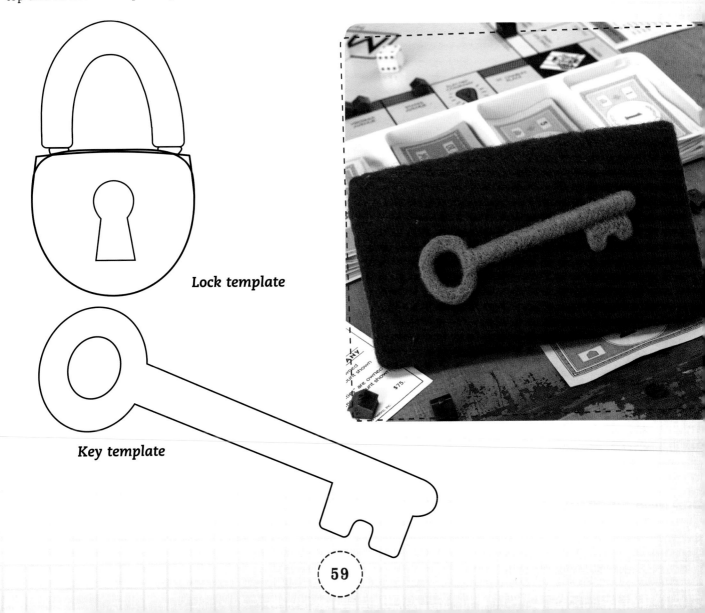

**Lock template**

**Key template**

# MOLDY COZY

Artists are often inspired by the things that surround them in life. If you live at the beach, you might paint the ocean. Folks who work in offices may write short stories about the secret and deadly paper cut tournaments happening in the mail room. If you're me, you might make a cozy for your phone inspired by the green stuff that lives in the refrigerator where edible food should be, but isn't, because you still haven't figured out how to be a grown-up.

## Materials & Tools

wool fiber in a variety of greens and mold colors/textures

foam

1 multi-needle felting tool

1 single felting needle

hook and eye clasp

thread

sewing needle

## 1. Make a base

Make flat fabric 10" × 6" (25.5cm × 15cm) with dark green fiber (see Creating Flat Fabric on page 13). The fabric should be roughly 3 times the length of your MP3 player or phone, allowing at least ½" (1.5cm) on each side for a seam allowance. Fold over and finish the top and bottom ends, making the flap-end asymmetrical and skewed.

## 3. Mold grows

Because mold comes in so many colors, this is a good chance to use your leftover scraps of fiber and fabric. Make some of it puffy, some of it stringy, all of it moldy. Reference photos of mold, pond scum or the gym shoes of a teenaged boy for inspiration.

## 2. Get moldy

Add bits and pieces of fiber to the surface of the fabric with a single felting needle. Work small patches at a time.

## 4. Seam it

Use a single needle to close the edges of the cozy (see Finishing Flat Fabric on page 16). Use extra bits of fiber to camouflage the seams and give the cozy an overall puffy, slimy-looking texture.

## 5. Add a clasp

Use a needle and thread to sew the hook and eye on the inside of the flap and cozy, making sure they line up well and that the cozy stays closed when hooked.

# STONED

Let the shiny, textured batt do the work when creating these geological treasures. String husky, angular stone-like beads together and you're wearing a necklace that shouts, "Look at me, everybody! I'm semi-precious!"

## Materials & Tools

wool fiber in dark blue

specialty fibers or batt with shiny contrasting colors and texture

foam

1 single felting needle

stretchy beading cord

embroidery thread needle with eye large enough to accommodate the stretchy cord

needle-nose pliers

scissors

2 small magnets

## 1. Make stones

Use a single needle to create an asymmetrical stone shape from the darker base color (see Felt a Ball on page 17). Before the stone is entirely finished, wrap it in a layer or two of the fancy fiber blend and continue felting until you're happy with the look and feel. Repeat, making each stone different, until you have enough to fit around the neck of your choice.

## 2. Cast the first stone

Thread the stretchy cord through the embroidery needle and tie a knot at the end. (The knots you tie should be big enough so they don't pull through the bead, but small enough so the knot doesn't sit on top of the stone. One or two overhand knots should do the trick.) Poke the needle through one end of a stone. Use the needle-nose pliers to carefully pull the needle through the other side.

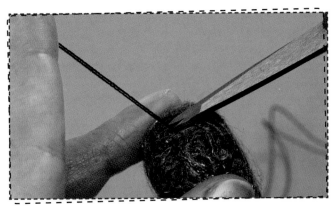

## 3. Hide the knot

Pull the stretchy cord so the knot is pulled about 1/16" (2mm) into the end of the stone. Trim the excess stretchy cord.

## 4. Finish stoning

Continue skewering and pulling stones onto the stretchy cord, place each stone against the next. After you string the last stone, tie a knot snug to the surface. Pull the last bead a bit to help hide the knot and trim the excess stretchy cord like you did in step 2.

## 5. Add the magnets

Glue a magnet to the end of the first and last rocks, over the stretchy cord knots. Let the glue dry completely and you are ready for your vacation to Roccapulco.

**Tip** It is possible to hide the magnets in the two end stones. Use stronger magnets and follow the same magnet technique detailed in the Katamari Damacy Magnetic Desk Toy on page 81.

# MORTARLESS MOSAIC PENDANT

This pin is a classy accessory that uses fiber for mortar. It also provides an amazing excuse to take a sledgehammer to your fine china.

## Materials & Tools

wool fiber in grey

foam

1 single felting needle

mosaic pieces

glue

pin back

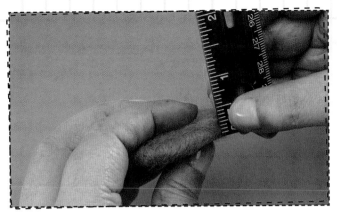

## 1. Make a base

Using the single needle, felt a base piece approximately ¼" (6mm) thick (see Felt a Puck on page 19). This piece is about 2¾" × 2¼" (7cm × 6cm).

## 2. Make with the mosaic-ing

Lay your mosaic pieces on the surface of the base, fitting the pieces together anyway you like but with about ¼"–½" (6mm–1.5cm) in between each one. Glue them to the base one at a time.

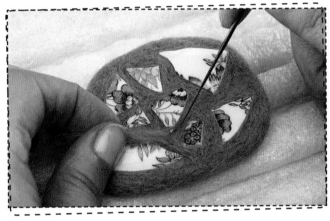

## 3. Felt as cement

After the glue dries, use loose fiber to slowly build up the felt between the pieces until finished. This is definitely a time for lots of thin layers and very careful, gentle pokes.

## 4. Add the pin

Place the mosaic face down and glue on the pin back. Allow the glue to dry.

## 5. Finishing touch

Make a small piece of flat fabric with fuzzy edges, wide enough to cover the inner par of the pin back. Felt the fabric over the pin back for strength and a clean finished look.

# RACE TRACK SKINNY SKARF

Inspired by road-themed play rugs for kids, I thought it'd be fun to wear the road around your neck while you ride the bus around town asking for transfers you're never gonna use.

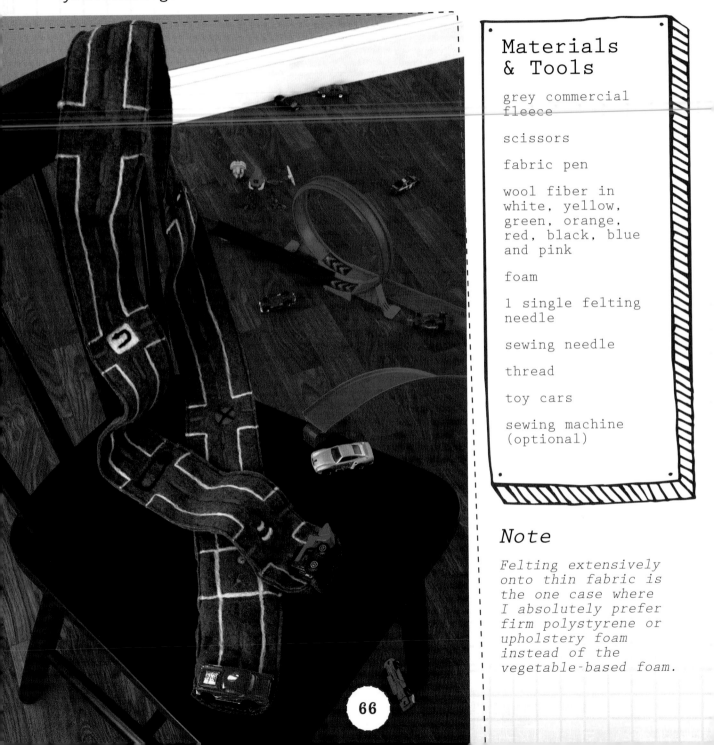

## Materials & Tools

grey commercial fleece

scissors

fabric pen

wool fiber in white, yellow, green, orange, red, black, blue and pink

foam

1 single felting needle

sewing needle

thread

toy cars

sewing machine (optional)

## Note

*Felting extensively onto thin fabric is the one case where I absolutely prefer firm polystyrene or upholstery foam instead of the vegetable-based foam.*

## 1. Road prep

Cut the fleece into two strips, about 4" (10cm) wide and as long as you choose. (This one is a super-duper 6' [2m] long.) Use a marker or fabric pen to draw the template for what will become the white road lines. Whether you measure or use a ruler is up to you, but freehanding the design is the key to how cute this skarf is.

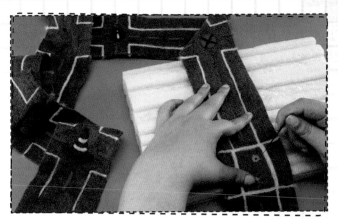

## 2. Road work

Using a single needle, felt all white lines first (see Embellishing on page 29). Next, use the various other wool fiber colors to add road signs, people's parks or road kill to each crosswalk and to the ends of the skarf.

## 3. Soft shoulder

Place your embellished fleece on top of its fleecy twin by running the edges through a sewing machine in one incredibly long rectangle, or sew it together with the needle and thread.

## 4. Shoulder work

Trim any excess fleece to make the edges neater. Straight lines are extremely unimportant.

## 5. Parking cars

Use the sewing needle and thread to secure the toy cars to each end of the skarf for fun and to add a bit of weight. If your car has space in the wheel wells all the way through, you can go around and around through there with your needle and thread. If it needs more securing, you can sew over the top of the car, like a seat belt.

# VOODOO DOLL EARRINGS

It's really about being prepared: If there's a fire, you need to have a fire extinguisher. When you cut your finger while dicing onions, you better have a Band-Aid. When you wake up to find that your roommate has stolen your change jar, consumed all the coffee and freed your hamster, tiny effigies of justice dangling from your ears are your only hope.

## Materials & Tools

wool fiber in white, black and red

foam

1 single felting needle

4 sewing pins with red heads

2 head pins

round-nose pliers

wire cutters

needle-nose pliers

ear wires

## Note

*For some projects, I like to keep the felt clean, so I pick out stray colored fibers as I come across them. But with a project like this, I leave strays alone to help give the finished piece a more natural look. Do you think voodoo mummies take lots of showers or something? Because, they don't. You are so silly.*

### 1. Doll parts

Use white fiber and a single needle to felt the doll body, arms, legs and head separately.

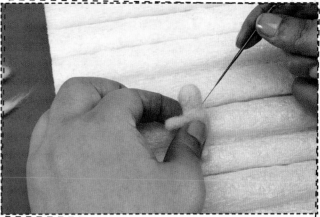

### 2. Body building

Use a single needle to felt the pieces into place (see Forming Attachments on page 23).

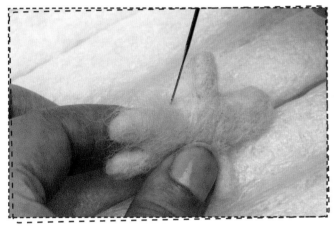

### 3. Build a little more bulk

Add a wisp or two around the body to further secure the parts, smooth out any seams and build a more voodoo-ish shape overall.

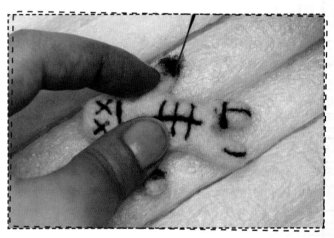

### 4. Make your marks

Use red and black fiber in teeny-weeny wisps to make details on the doll (see Embellishing on page 29).

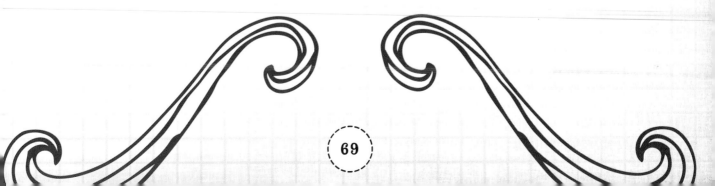

## 5. Prepare the pins

Use needle-nose pliers to bend the tips of the sewing pins. You can use wire cutters to trim the pins if they are too long.

## 6. Pin it down

As you imagine your boss in your mind's eye, slide the pins into place on the doll.

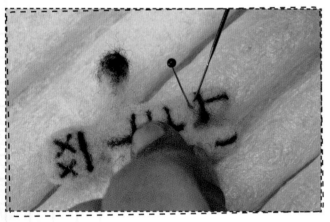

## 7. Extra pokes

Carefully felt around the pin insert point if needed to tighten things up. Use 2 pins per voodoo doll.

## 8. Prepare the skewer

Cut the tip of the head pin with wire cutters to make it sharper.

## 9. Prepare to be skewered

To make a hole big enough to fit the head pin, slowly push the felting needle all the way through the doll and remove. Be careful!

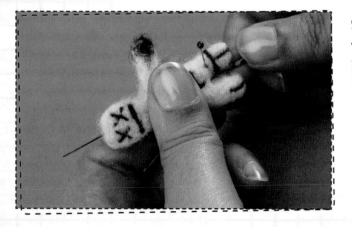

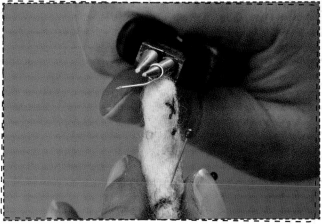

### 10. Commence skewering

Impale the doll on the head pin from crotch to head. If needed, use the needle-nose pliers to help pull the pin through.

### 11. Make a loop

Use the round-nose pliers to make a loop at the top of the doll.

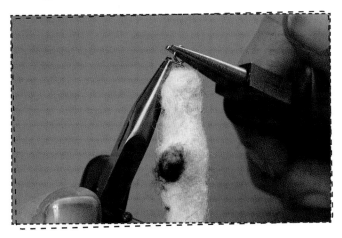

### 12. Wrap the loop

Grasp the loop in the round-nose pliers. Using the needle-nose pliers, wrap the wire tail around the base of the loop several times.

### 13. Attach the earring finding

Attach the ear wire to the loop at the doll's head.

# PLAYABLES

I don't think grown-ups get to play enough. Being silly, frolicking, making up stories, wiggling, giggling, flexing the imagination muscles; these are the activities that inspire big ideas, enhance our relationships, and simply make us feel alive. You like feeling alive, don't you? Sure, we all do!

# SHEEP OF THE DEAD FINGER PUPPET

Puppets can be therapeutic. This one was designed to help me work through my lingering feelings about the Barn Raising of the Undead I experienced as a child. Sure, he's kind of freaky looking and doesn't comfort me as much as saying "Braaaaaaiiiinnnnsssss" over and over again until I cry, but … remember, zombies are scary, and therapy takes time.

## Materials & Tools

merino wool fiber in olive green and moldy green

wool fiber in black, white and red

foam

1 multi-needle felting tool

1 single felting needle

screwdriver or other object to fit inside as a form

## 1. Build a body

Make a flat fabric (see Creating Flat Fabric on page 13) but only use 2 layers of fiber. Hold it over the screwdriver and gently poke it, first from the top down and then around the sides; this creates the base of the puppet (see Hard Objects on page 28). (When it's all done, your finger will go where the screwdriver is.)

## 2. Add bulk

Pull and twist some of both green fibers to mix the colors and make them tangle (see Color Blending on page 35). Wrap the fiber around the screwdriver on top of the flat fabric and gently poke it into place. With the felt still on it, turn the screwdriver upside down and felt it from underneath to tighten up the edges around the hole. Turn it right side up. Add more fiber as needed to bulk up the carcass until you have a puffy soft sock that fits over the screwdriver.

## 3. Go to pieces

Felt a moldy green squat log with a round end and a fuzzy end for the snout (see Felt a Log on page 21). Make two more logs for the arms, but this time make them longer and skinnier. Use more mixed green fiber and felt it to the fuzzy end of the snout to form the head, leaving the bottom fuzzy for attaching to the body. Felt a couple ears out of moldy green with olive green detailing.

## 4. Attached

Use a single needle to attach the ears to the head, the head to the top of the body and the arms to the sides of the body (see Forming Attachments on page 23). If needed, add more fiber around the neck to help strengthen and secure the head.

## 5. Face it

Refer to Embellishing on page 29 to build out his face. Use a bit of white fiber to form the still-in-the-socket eye to the snout, keeping it nice and bulgy. Use a tiny wisp of black around the edge of the eye to make it look extra rotten, and poke another tiny wisp of black right into the center of that eye. Attach the loose end of the red eye-cord to the head where the eye belongs. Make a flat black rectangle with rounded corners on the end of the head for the mouth with tiny wisps of black coming up for the nose. Use little bits of white fiber on top of the black rectangle to make the creepy sheepy teeth and add a pinch of red fiber where appropriate for the blooooooooood.

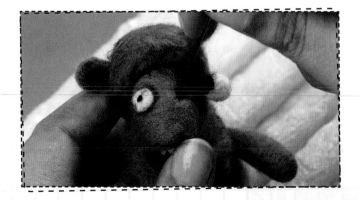

You just finished a quiet, candle-lit dinner for two and the mood is romantic. You gaze across the table into your lover's eyes, flutter your lashes and send that signal ... you know the one. It's unmistakable and he picks up your vibe right away. Without words you passionately sweep your arm across the table, clearing the dishes onto the floor in the heat of passion. He rises and struggles to whip out his ... homemade mancala board and sets up a game.

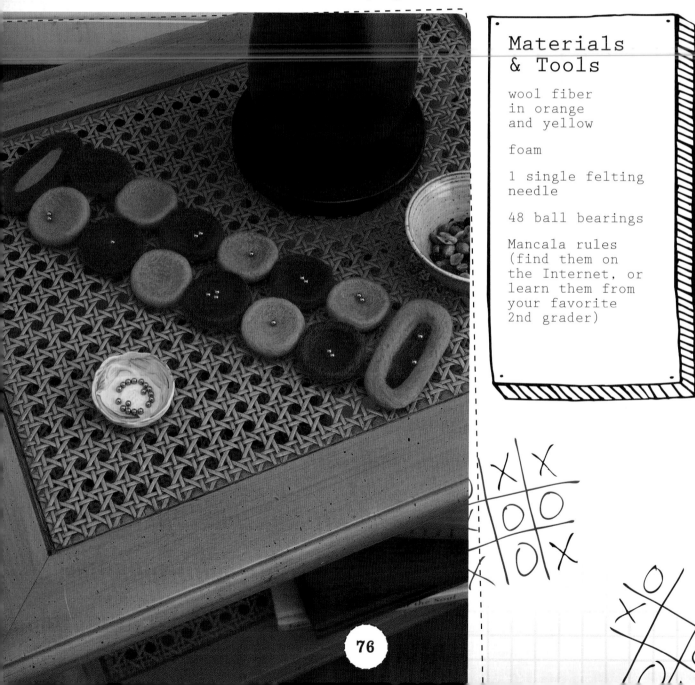

## Materials & Tools

wool fiber in orange and yellow

foam

1 single felting needle

48 ball bearings

Mancala rules (find them on the Internet, or learn them from your favorite 2nd grader)

## 1. Cup creations

Make 6 yellow and 6 orange cups of the same size; I made cups approximately 2" (5cm) in diameter. Start each cup with the puck instructions (see Felt a Puck on page 19) but, while the puck is still somewhat soft, focus poking inward toward the center to create a divot. Add fiber around the edge of the cup as needed to build up the sides.

Use the same technique for the yellow-and-orange end pieces but make them long instead of round, approximately 2" × 4" (5cm × 10cm). Hold the end pieces up to two of your cups to make sure the sizes fit together nicely. Once formed, poke a thin layer of the other color to the inside of each end piece for contrast.

Felt a total of 20 thick orange and yellow strips about 2" (5cm) long with fuzzy ends.

## 2. Back it up

Lay out the cups in two rows to be sure they will fit together properly, one after the other. Some cup irregularity is normal so just mix and match until the board sits the way you want it to. Connect the cups in pairs by felting a strip to the bottoms, being careful not to poke so far that the color comes through the other side.

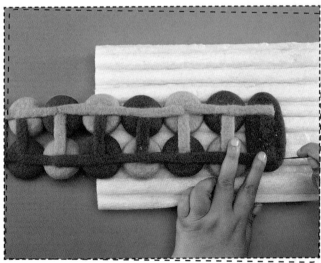

## 3. Making connections

Connect each paired set to the one next to it by felting the strips to the cup bottoms.

## 4. The ends

Finally, attach the long cups to each end by felting strips to the bottoms. Use the ball bearings as your playing pieces and remember: It's not cheating if you don't get caught.

# CIGGIE KITTY

Nobody should smoke and that includes kitties. But some kitties do have a green leafy substance that they adore. I know what to do: Let's stick some nip in this cigarette and watch the cats go crazy.

## Materials & Tools

wool fiber in tan, cream, grey and black

foam

1 multi-needle felting tool

1 single felting needle

catnip

piece of paper

capsule or container

bells or corn kernels

## Note

*Cats play hard; like a real cigarette, don't expect this one to last forever.*

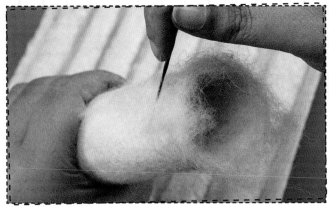

## 1. Make an empty ciggie

Felt a 6½" × 20" (16.5cm × 51cm) cream piece of fabric (see Creating Flat Fabric on page 13). Seam it as a tube with open ends (see Finishing Flat Fabric on page 16).

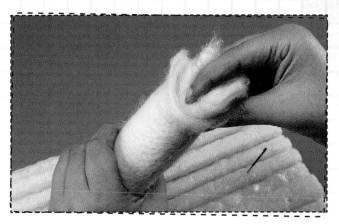

## 2. Plug it

Stuff a small plug of cream fiber in one end of the tube.

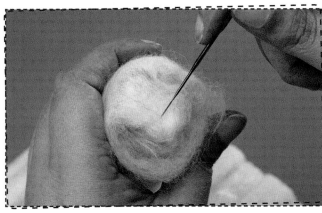

## 3. Seal it

Use a single needle to felt the plug into place. This will become the "mouth end."

## 4. Make a filtered tip

Felt some tan fiber around the mouth end in thin tufts to make the filter.

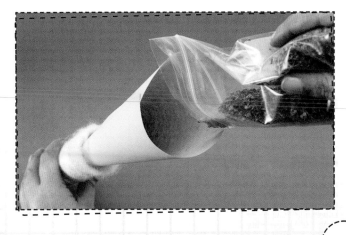

## 5. Fill 'er up

Stand the cigarette straight up, mouth end down. Using a piece of paper as a funnel for easier filling, pour a couple inches of catnip inside the empty cavity.

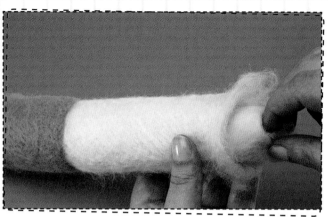

## 6. Put the jingle in the ciggie

Put some bells or corn kernels in the capsule and close it up. Shake it and make sure it sounds good to you. Drop the bell capsule inside the cigarette cavity. It will rest on top of the catnip.

## 7. Top it off

Stuff another nugget or two of cream fiber into the cavity as needed until the cigarette has about ½" (1.5cm) of fuzz at the end.

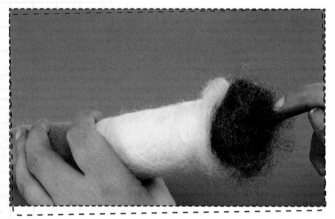

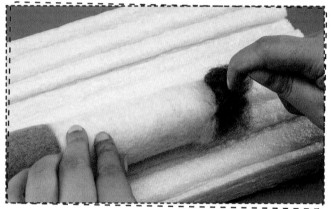

## 8. Ashes, ashes

Use some mixed grey and black fiber for the ashy ending and felt it into place (see Color Blending on page 35).

## 9. Seal it again

Put the cigarette on the foam and poke the fuzzy cream end into the grey ash plug until it's sealed all the way around.

# KATAMARI DAMACY MAGNETIC DESK TOY

Katamari Damacy (塊魂, *lit.* "Clump Spirit") is a bewitching, addictive Japanese video game that definitely deserves a needle-felted homage.

If you haven't been bitten by the KD bug, here's a quick rundown: You are a prince, sent to various locations by your disapproving, purple-tights-wearing dad, The King of All Cosmos. He commands you to push a very sticky ball around the universe, grabbing up all of the objects you can. Your ball is very tiny to begin with, but as you pick up thumbtacks, pieces of sushi, crayons, etc., it begins to grow until, eventually, you can roll up giant squid, Ferris wheels and even whole islands. Picture Sisyphus on an Ecstasy+Ritalin binge, as drawn by an 8-year-old girl and you pretty much have the idea. It's impossibly colorful, hilariously surreal, and now you can make a real life version of your very own.

## Materials & Tools

wool fiber in apple green, white, hot pink and tangerine

foam

1 multi-needle felting tool

1 single felting needles

6 neodymium magnets, approximately 12.6mm diameter, 5mm thick

strong glue (porous to non-porous)

miscellaneous small pieces of your universe

## Optional Shortcut Materials

foam ball, 1"-1½" (2.5cm-4cm) diameter

white commercial felt

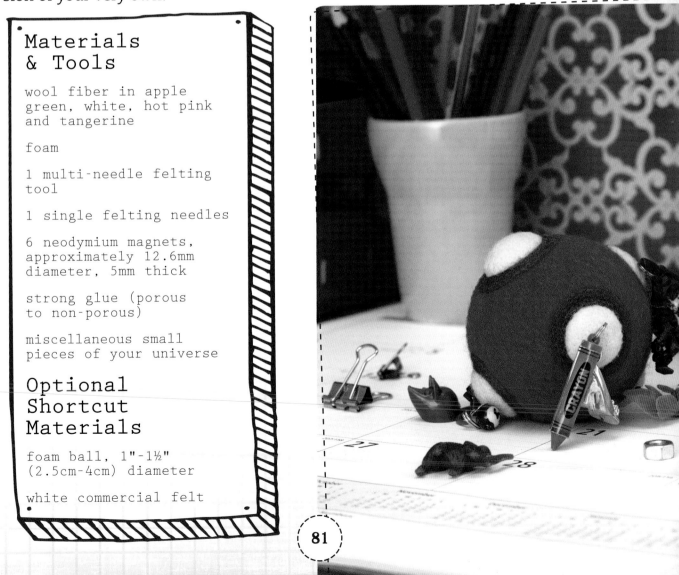

## 1. Attach the first two magnets

First, create a ball approximately 2½"–3" (6.5cm–7.5cm) diameter with the apple green fiber, either from scratch or using a foam base (see Felt a Ball on page 17 or Soft Objects on page 27).

Pick a starting point anywhere on the base. Glue the first magnet to the base, following any special instructions dictated by your glue of choice. Making sure the first magnet stays in place, glue the second magnet to the spot on the polar opposite side of the base and allow the glue to dry.

## 2. Attach the rest of the magnets

Turn the ball and repeat step 1, centering 2 new magnets, 1 between each of the previously added ones. Turn the ball so the previous magnets are horizontal to the table. After these are dry, repeat step 1 again, centering the last 2 magnets on the top and bottom of the ball.

## 3. Cover the magnets

Use a few layered tufts of white fiber to create a flat felt piece large enough to cover one magnet, or cut pieces of white commercial felt to size, approximately ¾" (2cm) in diameter (see Creating Flat Fabric on page 13). Place the flat piece over a magnet and poke around the fabric edge with a single felting needle to attach it to the base.

Using a single needle, continue gently poking around the magnet on all sides to secure the white felt, adding wisps of fiber as needed for coverage (see Hard Objects on page 28). Repeat this step until all of the magnets are securely covered.

## 4. Add color accents

Poke thin wisps of hot pink fiber around the edge of the white bumps to create an outline (see Embellishing on page 29). Use thin wisps of tangerine fiber around the edge of the hot pink to make the final outline. Repeat until all of your white bumps have colorful outlines.

## 5. Prepare the pieces

If some of your goodies aren't already magnetic, you can attach paperclips or jump rings as you see fit. You can glue magnets to some larger items to make them even more "attractive."

# MR. FAUX-TATO HEAD

This project is a great example of how templates can keep you sane. The Tater Man has more subtlety to his shape than you might think. You don't have to do what I did: study the potato head tribes in the jungles of Idaho for over three years. Seriously, I'm like the Jane Goodall of potato heads. Don't be like me; use the templates.

## Materials & Tools

wool fiber in brown, red, blue, white, black and green

foam

1 multi-needle felting tool

1 single felting needle

templates

pipe cleaners or craft wire

14 neodymium magnets, approximately 12.6mm diameter, 5mm thick

strong glue (porous to non-porous)

## Optional Shortcut Materials

foam ball or cone

## Note

*Neodymium magnets are incredibly powerful. They can hurt you if they snap together so watch your fingers. Keep them, and your finished project, away from your cell phone, computer, floppy discs and robotic vacuuming machines.*

## 1. Make a potato

Start a ball from scratch or around a foam base (see 3D Part I: Shapes on page 17 or Soft Objects on page 27). Add layers of brown fiber around the base and build up the shape of the potato. Use the template as a guide. Add more fiber in the thicker areas and poke more in areas that indent. You are sculpting ... sculpting a potato.

## 2. Make accessories for potato play time

Use the template to create some eyes with the black and white fiber and shoes in blue, and your imagination for the nose, mouth and hairdo. Don't stop with the parts shown here. There's no reason not to sew your tater a hoodie. Make him some tots. Live a little!

## 3. Arm your potato

Make two felt logs with the pipe cleaners or craft wire inside, fuzzy on one end and with a round hand base on the other (see Making an Armature on page 25). Felt the fingers separately as little rounded logs and felt them into the hands. Use the template for reference.

Add some white fiber around the base of the hand and lightly poke it into place to create the glove base.

## 4. Attach the arms

Slide the bit of wire on the fuzzy end of the arm into the body. Use a single needle to felt the fuzzy end of the arms into the sides.

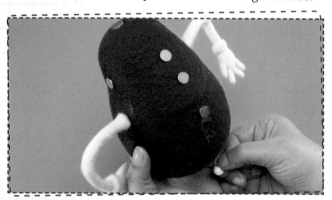

## 5. Add the magnets

Glue the magnets into place on the body where you would connect the hair, ears, eyes, nose, mouth and shoes.

## 6. Add more magnets

Glue magnets to the corresponding body parts, making sure the magnets face the right direction for polarity.

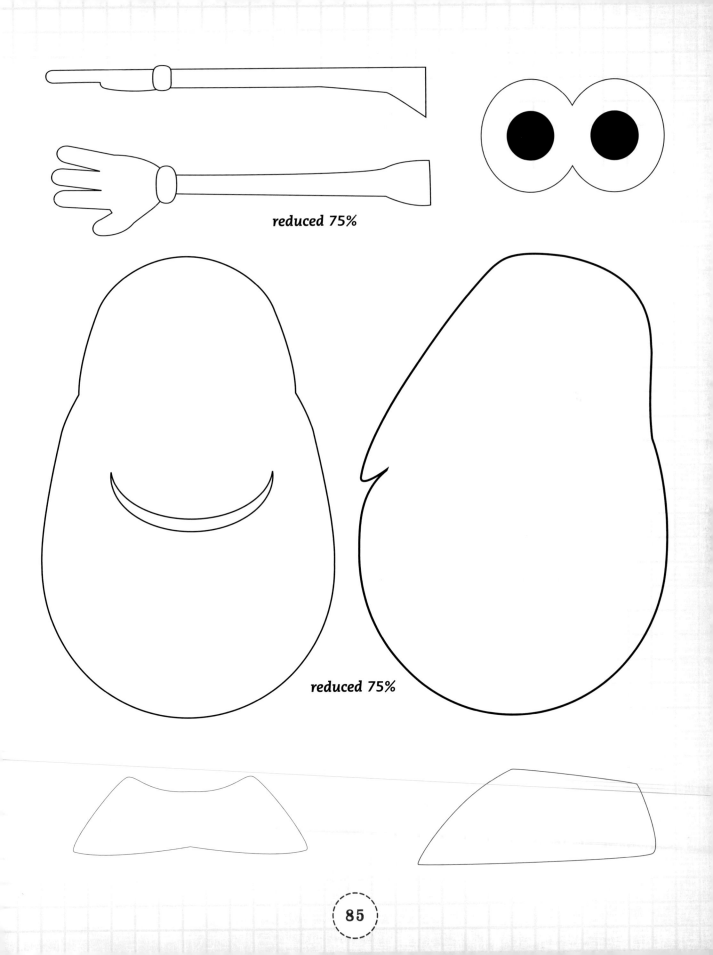

reduced 75%

reduced 75%

Yo-yo tricks have the best names. You've got your classic "Around the World" and your "Walk the Dog," but you've also got the "Worm Hole" and the "Over the Shoulder" and the astoundingly popular "Sucker Punch the Baby." OK, I totally made up that last one. Sorry.

## Materials & Tools

wool fiber in lilac, royal blue and turquoise

foam

1 single felting needle

yo-yo template

small, sharp scissors

screwdriver or chopstick

aluminum binding posts with screws, 2 1" (2.5cm) pieces and 1 ¼" (6mm) piece

washers that fit around the binding posts

yo-yo string

**Tip** *Aluminum binding screws are sometimes called "sleeve bolts." They are often used to bind large accounting ledgers and expandable photo albums. You can find them at the hardware store as well as the office supply store. You can even find them in your local craft store, typically called "post extenders" in the photo album aisle.*

### 1. Make half a yo

The yo-yo pieces are really giant pucks, larger on one end than the other, and with a depth of approximately 1" (2.5cm). Use lilac fiber and a single felting needle to felt two dense pucks (see Felt a Puck on page 19). Use the template to make them as uniform as possible to avoid wobbling during play.

### 2. Add details

Use long, thin wisps of turquoise to make the swirly, starting in the center of the puck (see Embellishing on page 29). Repeat the process with royal blue fiber following the outside of the turquoise swirly.

### 3. Make a hole

Use the small, sharp scissors to carefully puncture a hole straight through the center of each yo-yo piece.

### 4. Make the hole bigger

Insert the screwdriver or chopstick into the hole to make it large enough for the binding posts.

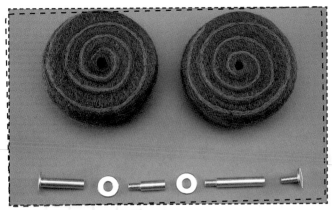

### 5. Behold the hardware

This photo shows you the order of the screw pieces and washers. When screwed together, the pieces measure approximately 2¼" (5.5cm) in total length.

### 6. Add the first screw piece

Starting with the binding post on the left in step 5, insert the piece into the first yo-yo piece so the flat end rests against the center of the swirl.

## 7. Screw again

Put the washer on the end of the next screw piece.
Attach this to the first screw piece.

## 8. And again

Attach the last two screw pieces to each other and
slide them into the second yo-yo piece so the flat end
rests against the center of the swirl.

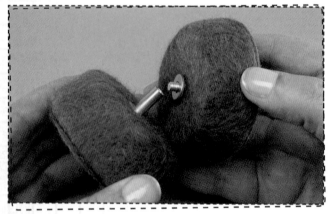

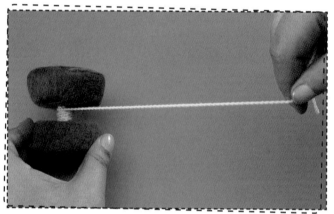

## 9. And one more time

Screw the yo-yo pieces together with the second
washer between them so the second washer keeps the
second yo-yo piece held securely.

## 10. Add the string

There are special tips and tricks for attaching yo-yo
strings to get the best results. Follow the instructions
on your string package, or see Resources on page 142.

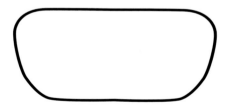

The story I'm about to unfold takes place in the early morning. You sit at your desk trying to focus, but it's Monday and you are not, in the parlance of our time, feeling it. You notice your colleagues are working hard. Well, harder than you are. They are achievers and proud we are of all of them, but you are not ready to settle into your workday. You set the bowling pins on your desk as the boss comes around the corner, demanding to know what you're doing. You answer, "Obviously, you're not a golfer," take a deep breath and roll.

## Materials & Tools

wool fiber in white, red and black

foam

1 single felting needle

template

10 ½" (1.5cm) metal washers

1 ½" (1.5cm) marble

strong glue (porous to non-porous)

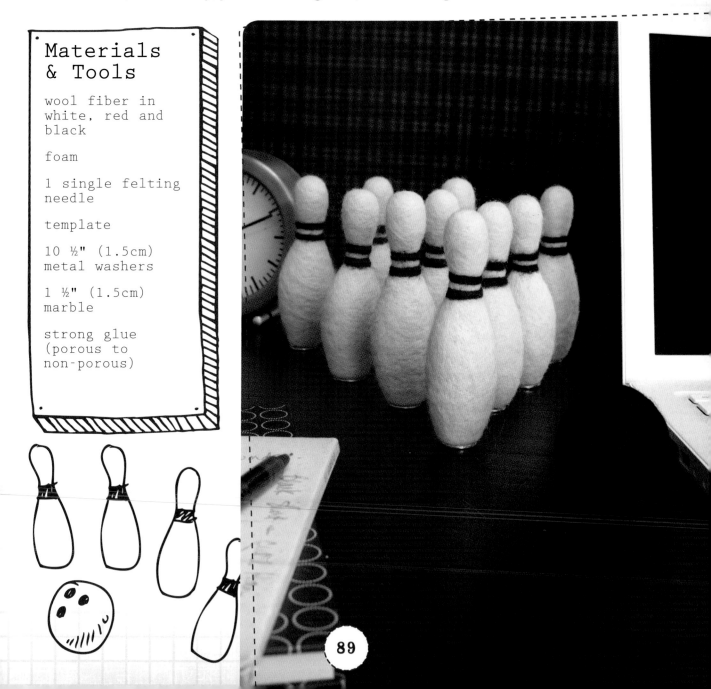

## 1. Make a bowling pin base

Create a white log with fuzzy ends, approximately 3" (7.5cm) long and ¼" (6mm) in diameter (see Felt a Log on page 21). Fold one fuzzy end down over the log and felt around it. This will become the top of the pin.

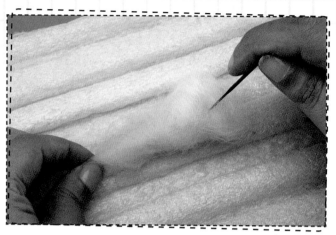

## 2. Build up the pin shape

Add tufts of fiber up and down the log as needed to form the bowling pin. Repeat until you have 10 white bowling pins.

**Tip** *Examine the pin from all sides as you work, holding it to the template often to keep the pin as uniform as you can, if you're into the whole "symmetry" thing.*

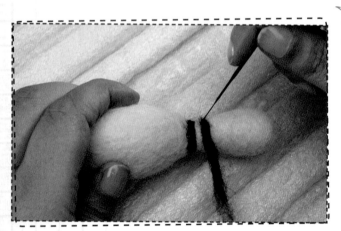

## 3. Add stripes

Poke thin wisps of red fiber around the neck of each pin (see Make a Stripe, Straight Up on page 29). Holding them up to the template will help you make sure the stripes stay consistent on each pin.

## 4. Attach washers

Glue one washer to the bottom of each bowling pin and allow the glue to dry. The washers will help the pins sit up straight on your desk and make knocking them down a little more challenging.

## 5. Make the bowling ball

Use black fiber to felt around the marble to approximately 2" (5cm) in diameter (see Hard Objects on page 28). The marble adds just enough weight to give your roll gusto. Poke 3 deep indents into the ball to create the finger holes. If the ball becomes less round after your indents, give the whole surface some more poking and add wisps of fiber where needed to polish the shape.

### Additional Ideas

- *Felt or embroider your friend Donny's name on the ball.*
- *Make several balls, in different colors and styles.*
- *Use different size marbles or lopsided objects inside the ball.*
- *Use larger washers to make the game harder.*
- *Needle felt a line to lay down on the desk. Don't cross over it when you roll or you'll have to mark it zero, dude.*

Behind the scenes author fun fact: I made this creature at around 3 o'clock in the morning. I was alone in the studio, hopped up on coffee, and I think this little maniac is wearing exactly the same facial expression I had on at the time.

## Materials & Tools

fabric pen or pencil

cardstock

template

2 pieces of pink felt fabric, commercial or handmade

pins

scissors

sewing needle

thread

fiber scraps for stuffing

plastic squeaker

wool fiber in white, black, green, pink

foam

1 single felting needle

## 1. Skin your monster

Use the included template or draw your own monster outline and cut it out; include a seam allowance of at least ¼" (6mm). Pin the template along the edge to the two pieces of felt. Cut around the template.

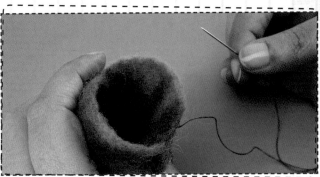

## 2. Sew the body

Place the two pieces of monster skin together facing front to front. Sew around the edges leaving about a 1" (2.5cm) hole.

## 3. Flip the body

Turn the monster carcass inside out through the hole. Use the eraser end of a pencil to gently push the body through itself until it's right-side-out.

## 4. Add stuffing

Use fiber scraps for stuffing a little at a time to fill the monster carcass. Use the pencil to push the filling into the nooks and crannies until the carcass is about half full.

## 5. Prepare the squeaker

Wrap the squeaker loosely in fiber stuffing, being careful not to completely cover the air hole.

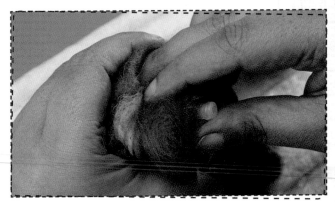

## 6. Insert the squeaker

Stick the wrapped squeaker inside the carcass, nozzle side up.

## 7. Finish filling

Fill the rest of the monster with more stuffing until he's all full and nauseous.

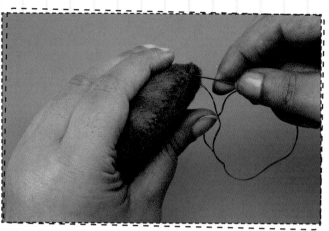

## 8. Close up the carcass

Use whatever stitch you love best to close the seam. It doesn't matter if it's visible because you're going to cover it up.

**Tip**

*If you would rather not felt the seam, use a blind stitch to close it nice and pretty.*

## 9. Color matching

Since the monster carcass felt is a special color, you want to use the scraps of felt to get a matching color fuzz for the bottom seam. Pluck at the pink felt fabric scraps to get a couple pinches of fiber tufts.

## 10. Cover the seam

Place the plucked fuzzies over the visible seam and use a single needle to poke the fibers to cover the seam.

**Tip**

*This plucking technique is good for spot color matching, accents and cover-ups but is not recommended for building an entire piece.*

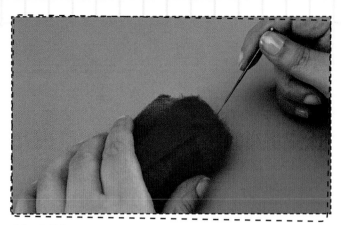

## 11. Add accents

Use the green fiber and a single needle to poke a long triangle from the base of his back to the tip of his forehead, creating a stripe and a forbidding widow's peak (see Embellishing on page 29). Use the same green for the horn tips.

 **Tip** *When adding accent details, use very shallow pokes to avoid piercing the squeaker within.*

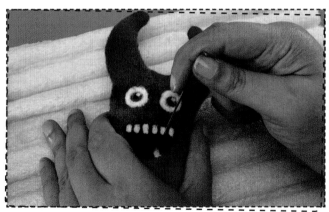

## 12. Make a funny face

Use a single needle to give your monster a face (see Embellishing on page 29). For the eyes, start with the white background then add the black pupil to the center. Use a tiny wisp of pink around the pupil to create the iris and, finally, add a tiny bit of white on top to make a highlight in the eye. For the mouth, first felt the black, then add little bits of white for each tooth.

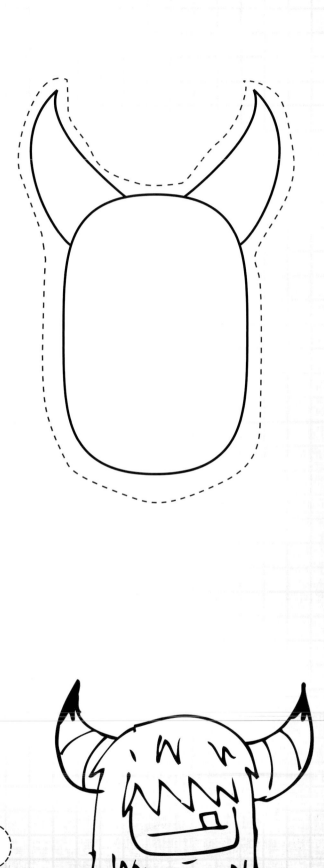

# TENTACLE TWISTIES

Call it eerily whimsical or hilariously frightening, but I like the idea that there might be wiggly creatures of all kinds lurking beneath the surface of what we see every day. This project helps bring that alarmingly wondrous or marvelously wicked concept to life.

## Materials & Tools

wool fiber in teal, green, orange and yellow

foam

1 multi-needle felting tool

1 single felting needle

pipe cleaner or craft wire

wire cutters

adhesive hook-and-tape dots or rubber suction cup

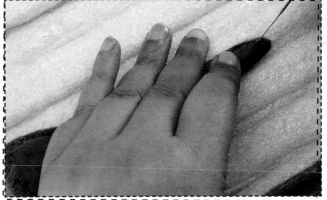

## 1. Make a base

Use the teal fiber around the pipe cleaner or craft wire to build a tentacle base (see Making An Armature on page 25). As you add fiber, add more around the bottom to make it wider than the tentacle tip. After the tentacle base is built up, use extra pokes to flatten the inside surface of the tentacles and flatten the bottom end.

## 2. Add color detail

Using a single needle or two, add green fiber detail to the flat inside of the tentacle (see Embellishing on page 29).

## 3. Add suction cups

Take a tiny wisp of orange and felt a ball on the inside base of the tentacle, using tiny pokes to keep it a little puffy (see Poke-a-Dot, Puffy Style on page 34). Use extra pokes in the center of the ball to create the puckered look of the suction cups. Take a teeny weeny bit of yellow fiber and poke it into the center of the sucker. Repeat this process, making the dots smaller and smaller as you work towards the tip of the tentacle.

## 4. Stick it

Decide where and how you want to play with your tentacle. If you want to be able to stick it to a wall or computer, adhesive hook-and-tape dots work nicely. Stick one piece of the hook-and-tape to the fat end of the tentacle and the other piece of hook-and-tape wherever you want the tentacle to stick. You can add more dots around other surfaces whenever you want to stick the tentacle someplace new. For glass, mirrors or any other slick surfaces, use a suction cup.

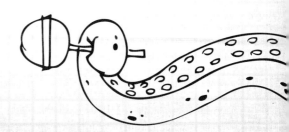

# BOBBLEHEAD BFF

Hiring people to listen to you talk is so expensive nowadays, and your family and friends all claim to have "other plans." The solution is to make yourself a new best friend whose entire purpose in life is to nod and genuflect as you go on and on and on and on and on and ...

## Materials & Tools

wool fiber in lavender, smoky purple, white and black

foam

1 single felting needles

templates

spring or craft wire and pliers

## Optional Shortcut Materials

foam ball

**Tip**

*The spring you choose will depend on the size and density of your finished bunny head. It should be long enough to keep the head from touching the body, but not so long that the head tips over. It should be thick enough that it keeps the head balanced, but not so thick that it's rigid and refuses to bobble.*

## 1. Make the bunny head

Start a ball from scratch or around a foam base, (see Felt a Ball on page 17 or Soft Object on page 27). Add layers of fiber around the base and build up the shape of the head. Before it's too solid, use extra pokes on the bottom of the ball to create a space for the spring to fit inside. Continue to add layers of fiber to thicken the head, making sure to continue felting the indent in the bottom.

## 2. Make the bunny parts

Use a single needle to create the bunny's body, arms, ears and feet (see 3D Part I: Shapes on page 17), using the templates if you want help with the shapes. Add a tuft of lavender fiber to the top of the bunny body to form a sort of neck that the spring can fit around. Use smoky purple to detail the bunny belly and the inside of the ears (see Embellishing on page 29).

## 3. Make the bunny face

Use a single needle or two and a wisp of white fiber to make the bulbous eyes. Use a little black for the pupils. Add black in a thin line for a smirky mouth and a little white for a pointy tooth (see Embellishing on page 29).

## 4. Put the pieces together

Use a single needle to connect the ears to the head and the arms and feet to the body. Attach the ears so they are solid enough to stay on, but wobbly enough that they move a bit when the head gets bouncy (see Forming Attachments on page 23).

## 5. Add the spring

Twist one end of the spring into the base of the head. If needed, felt some extra fiber around it for stability.

## 6. Add the head to the body

Fit the other end of the spring onto the neck piece so it fits snuggly. Felt some extra fiber around it if necessary for stability.

**Tip**

*If you have the spring in and it works great but the head is so heavy that the body tips over, glue a metal washer to the underside of the body to give the whole thing more stability.*

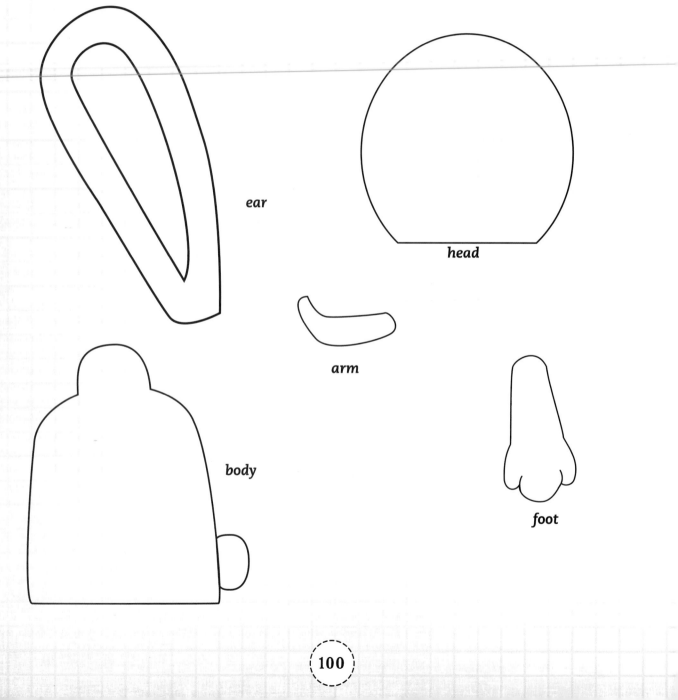

*ear*

*head*

*arm*

*body*

*foot*

# TORCHED

Fiber fire is just as fun, but infinitely safer than traditional fire: it's fuzzier, never goes out and is guaranteed not to turn you into human bacon.

## Materials & Tools

3 wooden dowels

hand drill or Dremel with drill bit, at least ¼" (6mm)

acrylic paint in black and silver

paintbrush

wool fiber in blue, purple, black, red, orange and yellow

foam

1 multi-needle felting tool

1 single felting needle

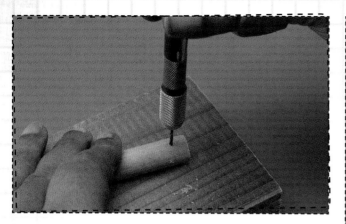

## 1. Prepare the dowels

Use a hand drill or Dremel to make a hole through each dowel near the top, large enough for the felting needle to fit through.

## 2. Decorate the dowels

Paint each dowel black and use silver paint for the tips. Allow the paint to dry.

**Tip** *While the black paint is still wet, poke a pin through the hole you drilled in step 1 to keep it from closing up.*

## 3. Start an anchor

Take a long thin wisp of black or blue fiber and gently poke it through the hole in the dowel so it sticks out on both sides.

## 3. Add to the anchor

Lay the dowel against the foam and felt some additional fiber to the wisps to thicken them. You don't want them to be stiff, just puffy and slightly felted together.

## 5. Finish the anchor

Wrap the puffy anchor pieces around the top of the dowel and lightly felt them to tack them down (see Hard Objects on page 28).

## 6. Add fiber and shape it up

Use a blend of black, blue and purple fiber (see Color Blending on page 35) to wrap around the top of the dowel and felt into place. Felt from all directions, making sure to incorporate the anchor pieces as you poke. Keep adding layers of fiber and poking until it is firm and round like a marshmallow. Turn the dowel upside down and felt the marshmallow from below to help achieve the desired shape.

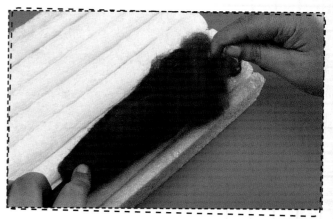

## 7. Start a fire

Use big tufts of red and orange fiber, wrapping them around the top of the marshmallow and making sure that some of the blue/black/purple shows at the bottom. Lightly poke the fire fiber into place, securing it to the marshmallow but not so much that it loses its wavy, bulgy texture.

## 8. Add more fire

Continue adding red, orange and now yellow fiber, keeping it extra wispy and asymmetrical at the top.

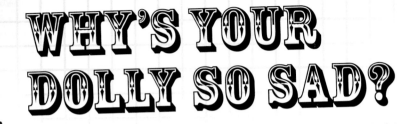

# WHY'S YOUR DOLLY SO SAD?

This doll has mood, but no face. She doesn't have to be frowning for us to know that she thinks school is boring, no one understands her, and that as soon as she has saved up her babysitting money, she's on a bus outta this suburban nightmare, like, ASAP.

## Materials & Tools

wool fiber in white, black, eggplant and red

foam

1 multi-needle felting tool

1 single felting needle

templates

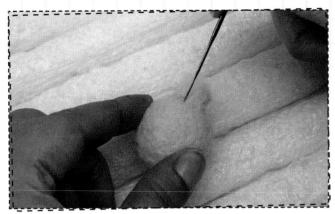

## 1. Make a bald head

Use white fiber to make a ball with some extra white at the base for a neck (see Felt a Ball on page 17 and Forming Attachments on page 23).

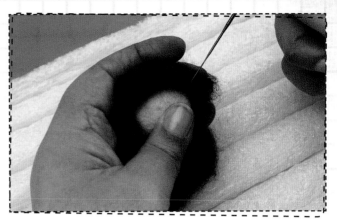

## 2. Add some hair

Using the eggplant fiber, make a thin lightly felted piece of fabric, double the length and width of the head (see Creating Flat Fabric on page 13). Hold the felt over the head ball and poke it into place. Lightly tug it where needed to create bangs, and add more fiber if needed for further shaping.

## 3. Make a body

Use the template to create the doll body in black fiber (see 3D Part I: Shapes on page 17). Add a thin felted piece around the bottom to form the skirt and some white fiber at the top to create the neckline (see Embellishing on page 29).

## 4. Make the inner skirt

Lightly felt a tuft of red fiber and use a single needle to attach it around the inside of the skirt to create the lining.

## 5. Make legs

Make a black log with one fuzzy end (see Felt a Log on page 21). Add extra black to the bottom of the log for boots. Add thin white wisps for stripey details.

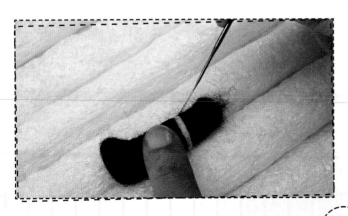

## 6. Attach the legs

Attach the legs to the bottom of the torso inside the skirt (see Forming Attachments on page 23).

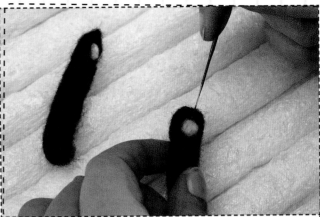

## 7. Make the arms

Make a black log with one fuzzy end. Felt a small white ball and attach it to the finished end of the arm. Felt a thin, tiny piece of black felt with a round edge and attach it to the arm around the outside of the hand to create a long sleeve.

## 8. Attach the arms

Use a single needle or two to poke the fuzzy end of the arm into place at the top of the doll. Add wisps of fiber as needed to secure the shoulder into place.

## 9. Attach the head

Poke the neck piece into the top of the torso. Be sure to hold the head at an angle so it faces down a bit, giving her the bona fide emo sadness she needs.

# FORM NOT FUNCTION

It's easy in the course of an ordinary day to stop seeing a great deal of what surrounds us. Creating *objet d'art* from a common object can be a welcome opportunity for me to consider and reconsider its shape, use and meaning.

# WALL TAPESTRY

Normally I'm not a fan of coloring within the lines—that's just what the man wants you to do! However, in this case, it's different. I love the vibrant, textured look you get from this technique; it reminds me of velvet paintings, but even fuzzier. Use the fabulous illustrations by artist Demian Parker on page 112, or try some of your own.

## 1. Transfer the design

Copy and enlarge one of the provided templates or print your own illustration to the size you desire. Lay out the commercial felt onto the work surface. Layer the transfer paper and then the illustration onto the felt. Use the pencil to trace the illustration outlines, transferring the image onto the felt.

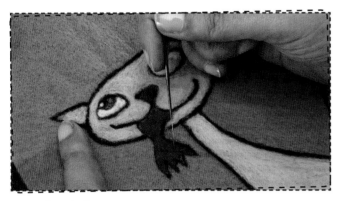

## 3. Color it in

Use small tufts of ice blue to fill in the design. Work in small patches and add fiber to make the fill smooth and even. Do the same with the white, green and orange for the eyes and fish details.

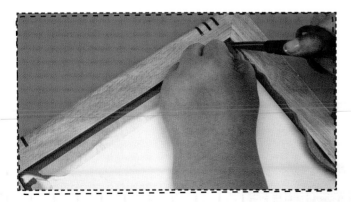

## 2. Create outlines

Use thin wisps of black fiber and a single needle to felt along the design and make the outline (see Embellishing on page 29).

## 4. Secure the felt

Remove the back of the frame, place the image face down with the matte board on top. Pull the sides of the felt that stick out as you press the matte board into place so the picture becomes taut in the frame. Tape the sides of the felt to the back of the matte board.

**Tip** *I got my frame at a thrift store. High five!*

## 5. Make adjustments

Trim the corners of the felt and, if needed, any other parts that will prevent the back of the frame from fitting properly.

### Note

*Felting extensively onto thin fabric is the one case where I absolutely prefer firm polystyrene or upholstery foam over eco foam.*

### 6. Back it up

Secure the frame back into place with whatever clips or attachments the frame came with.

### 7. Finishing touch

Turn the frame over and use a thin metal ruler or a piece of heavy cardstock to tuck any loose edges under the frame and to smooth any wrinkles.

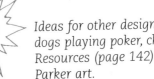
**Tip** *Ideas for other designs: abstract shapes, dogs playing poker, children's art. See Resources (page 142) for more Demian Parker art.*

*Enlarge the images as needed to fit your felt and frame*

# SMOKE UP, JOHNNY

I think smoking is yucky, but I think having a felted cigarette and ashtray on your coffee table to make people do double takes in astonishment is most excellent.

## Materials & Tools

wool fiber in aqua, grey, black, camel, red and white

foam

1 single felting needle

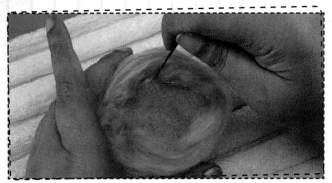

## 1. Build the base

Use a thick tuft of aqua fiber and the single needle to felt a round puck about 3" (7.5cm) in diameter.

Add lengths of fiber around the edges of the puck to build up the side wall, first felting from the top. As the sides begin to gain mass, poke all over to refine the shape.

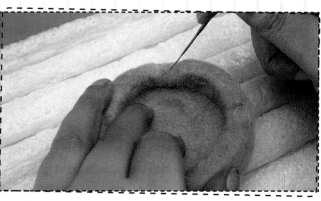

## 2. Ciggie divots

Before the sides get too solid, use extra pokes in 4 spots on the top of the edges to make indents for cigarette rest spots.

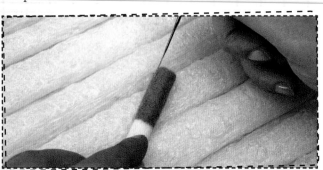

## 3. Make a cigarette base

Use white fiber and a single needle to make a thin-ish log with finished ends, about 2¾" (7cm) long (see Felt a Log on page 21). Add camel fiber in small wisps around the mouth end for a filter.

## 4. Finish the mouth end

Poke the camel fiber from the top as well as the sides. If needed, add a teeny-tiny wisp of white fiber to the center to further define the look of a cigarette filter.

## 5. Make some ash

Mix up a tiny tuft of black and grey fiber and poke it into the "lit" end to make the ashes. Take a small wisp of red and poke it to the center of the ashes to create an ember.

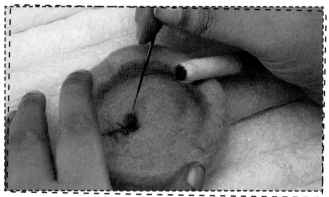

## 6. Add ashes to the ashtray

Place the finished cigarette in the ashtray to see where the lit end falls. Use a wisp of black/grey mix and felt it onto the ashtray in that spot.

# TEACH YOUR CHILDREN WELL

I heard once that the children are our future, which is kind of frightening because they really don't know a whole lot of stuff yet. This mobile starts the education process early, letting the kids in on the hazards and pitfalls that life can often present.

## Materials & Tools

templates

cardstock

scissors or craft knife

foam

wool fiber in red, orange, yellow, green, black and white

1 single felting needle

sewing pins

fishing line

sewing needle

mobile base

glue

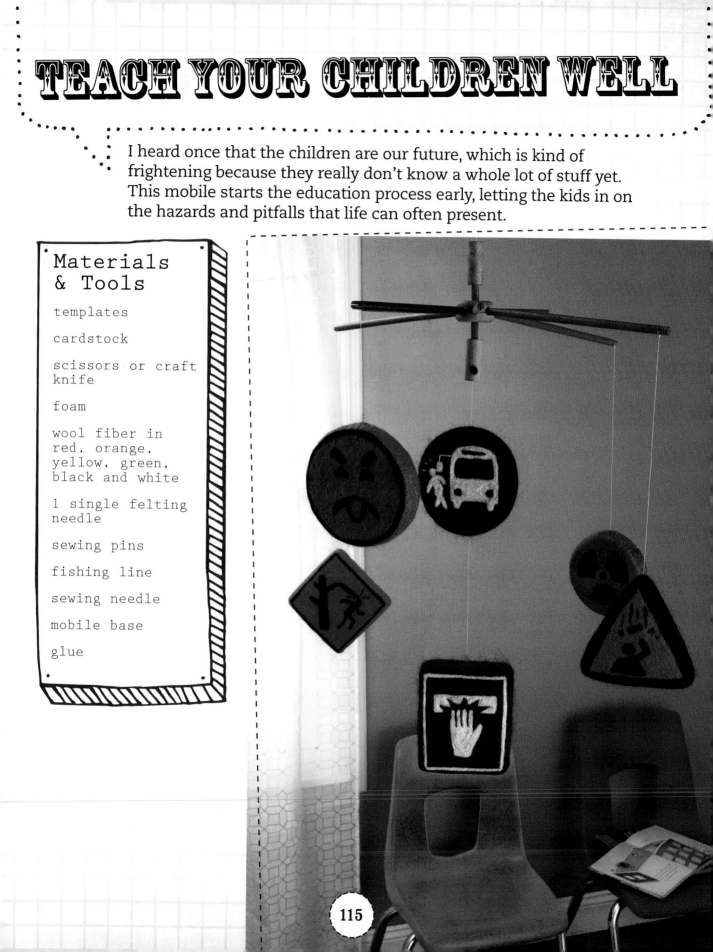

## 1. Prep the templates

Because the awesomeness of these images depends so much on clean lines and detailing, this project calls for templates. Print the templates on cardstock and cut each one around its outside edge. Use the craft knife or scissors to cut out the shapes leaving the rest of the template entirely intact. You're making a stencil.

## 2. Make the bases

Each piece of the mobile is basically a large puck. Start with a hunk of fiber (any color you want) and use a single needle to create the shape (see Felt a Puck on page 19). Add fiber around the base as needed to build bulk and size. Use the corresponding template to gauge the finished size of each piece.

## 3. Fill in the design

Lay the template on top of the finished puck and use the sewing pins to tack the template down securely, especially around the inside edges of the cutout.

Use small wisps of black or white fiber inside the template design and poke them into place (see Embellishing on page 29). Add more fiber in small wisps as needed and fill in the entire design, making sure to keep within the edges as cleanly as possible.

## 4. Finish the design

When finished filling in the template, remove it and give the whole design another poking over, as needed, for cleanup.

## 5. String up the pieces

Cut 12" (30.5cm) length of fishing line. String the needle with the fishing line and tie a knot at the end, big enough that it won't pull all the way through the puck. Pierce the puck from the back at an angle and come up through the top of the piece. This helps ensure that it will hang straight.

## 6. Trim the line

Pull the fishing line through the piece. Tug on the line to pull the knot into the piece snuggly, but not all the way through. Trim the excess fishing line. Repeat this step for each piece of the mobile.

## 7. Put it all together

Constructing a balanced mobile is different each time depending on the weight of the pieces and the type of hanging materials you use. The key is to build from the bottom rung up, balancing each tier independently and then attaching the balanced section to the one above. Tie the piece to the mobile base with the fishing line where needed and trim the excess line. Do this for each piece, and make sure the entire mobile balances before using a drop of glue at the hanging points to keep them in place.

**Tip** *I used a vintage Tinker Toy set to hang my mobile, but you can use whatever you like: hangers, wood dowels, craft wire—anything that you can securely tie the fishing line to and would love to see twirl around above your head.*

Templates have been reduced by 50 percent. Enlarge the images as needed.

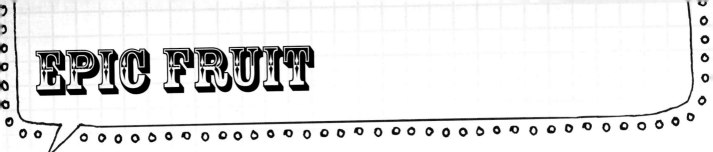

# EPIC FRUIT

Cherries are little bites of juicy deliciousness with taste much bigger than their size indicates. That's why this cherry is so enormous. Oh, and hey ... don't eat this cherry, OK?

## Materials & Tools

wool fiber in red and light green

foam

1 multi-needle felting tool

1 single felting needle

pipe cleaners or craft wire

## Optional Shortcut Materials

foam ball

template

## 1. Make a cherry

Create a ball from scratch or around a foam base (see Felt a Ball on page 17 or Soft Object on page 27). Add fiber in tufts until the cherry is about as tall as you want it to be. Add fiber on the sides as needed to make it cherry-shaped. Make extra pokes in the top center to create the stem divot. Add fiber all over to smooth out the surface and hide any lines caused from adding previous tufts.

## 2. Make a stem

Use light green fiber and pipe cleaners to create the stem (see Making An Armature on page 25). Leave one end fuzzy, and add more fiber to the tip to build the plucked portion at the top of the stem.

## 3. Add the stem to the cherry

Use a single felting needle to attach the fuzzy end of the stem to the top center of the cherry (see Forming Attachments on page 23).

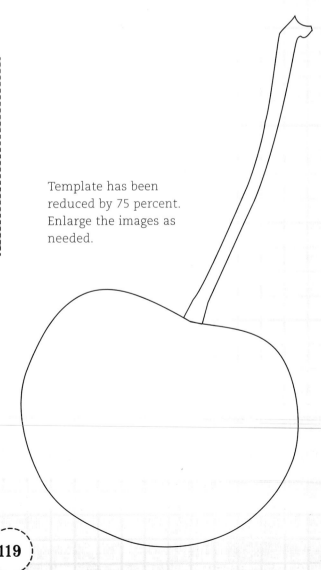

Template has been reduced by 75 percent. Enlarge the images as needed.

# SAY IT WITH NEON

Is anybody else living their life overwhelmed by the constant barrage of electronic highway billboards and empty advertising slogans, your mind all numb because of the endless drone of television sets in bars and restaurants, poorly designed store signage and all of the unnecessary exclamation points everywhere, and you look around into the dead eyes of the people around you at the supermarket and wonder what exactly is the point? Just me? Really?! Cool.

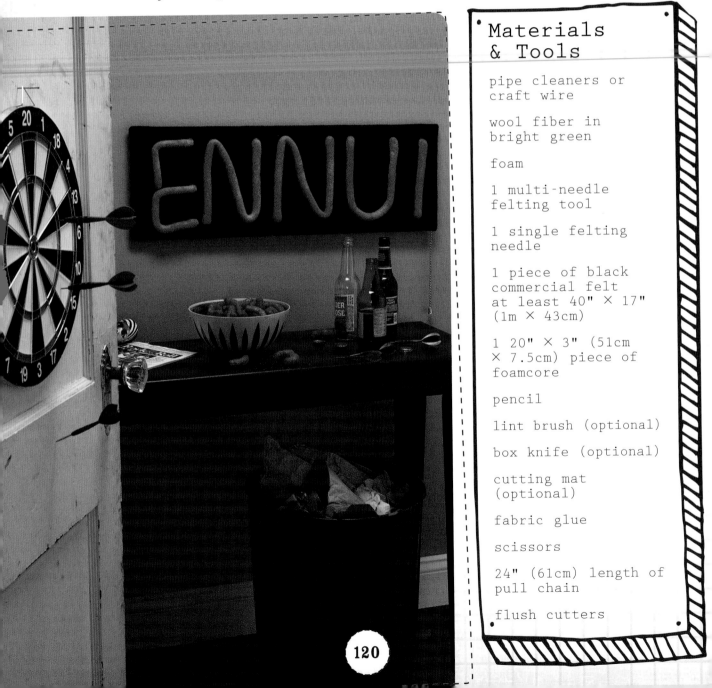

## Materials & Tools

pipe cleaners or craft wire

wool fiber in bright green

foam

1 multi-needle felting tool

1 single felting needle

1 piece of black commercial felt at least 40" × 17" (1m × 43cm)

1 20" × 3" (51cm × 7.5cm) piece of foamcore

pencil

lint brush (optional)

box knife (optional)

cutting mat (optional)

fabric glue

scissors

24" (61cm) length of pull chain

flush cutters

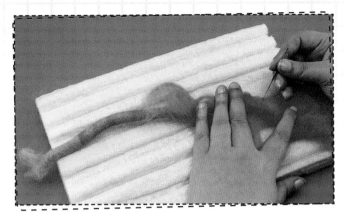

## 1. All about the armatures

To spell the word "ENNUI", make the following armature pieces out of bright green fiber and pipe cleaners, with an additional ¼" (6mm) of fuzzy ends (see Making An Armature on page 25). All pieces are approximately 1" (2.5cm) in diameter.

The E is made of two pieces: The first piece is 7" (18cm), the second piece is 11" (28cm); for the I, 7½" (19cm); for the U, 17" (43cm); and for the Ns, 24" (61cm).

## 2. Layout

Bend each piece into shape and lay them out on the commercial felt background. Don't worry if the pieces aren't holding their exact shape. Just make sure the whole word fits nicely on the background.

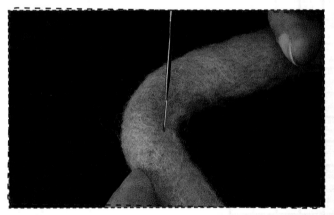

## 4. Shape the bends

Use extra pokes at the bends to further hold the shape of the E and to securely fasten the pieces to the background in several spots.

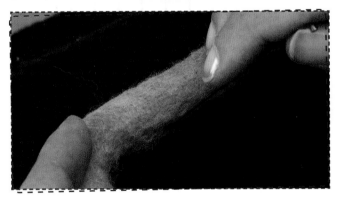

## 3. Attach the first letter

Slide foam underneath and, starting with the top of the E, use a single needle to poke along the edge, tucking the fiber towards the center of the armature and into the background.

## 5. Finish the ends

Poke the fuzzy ends of the E pieces from all sides to round them. This helps secure them but also furthers the neon illusion. Poke the very bottom edge of the rounded portion into the background to secure it.

## 6. Spell it out

Repeat for each piece until all the letters are in place. If needed, use a lint brush to clean the surface of the black felt.

## 7. Prep the board

Place the foamcore board under the black felt. Because I wanted a smaller background than the standard board size, I measured and marked the board, and cut it to size with a box knife and cutting mat. You can leave your background bigger or measure, mark and cut the board to your desired size.

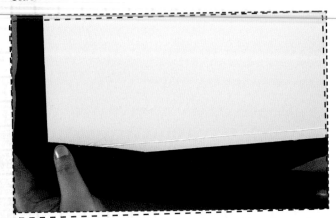

## 8. Attach the board

Center the word on the foamcore board. Turn the piece over (the top of the finished piece should be closest to you). Add a line of fabric glue to the bottom of the board. Fold the edge of the felt fabric up and over the foamcore, smoothing the fabric down with your hands. Allow the glue to dry according to the manufacturer's instructions.

## 9. Tailor the fabric

Use scissors to trim any excess fabric. Turn the piece so the bottom is closest to you. Add another line of glue to the edge of the foamcore board (the top of the finished piece). Pull the fabric taut and wrap it around to the back. Allow the glue to dry. Use the scissors to trim the excess fabric.

## 10. Tailor one end

Fold the fabric flap over the back of the board at the E end. Pull it taut and trim any excess fabric that bulges at the corners.

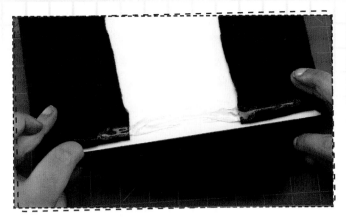

## 11. Finish attaching one end to the board

Add a line of glue to the edge of the board. Pull the fabric taut and wrap it around to the back. Smooth the fabric onto the glue and allow it to dry.

## 12. Arrange the chain

Before repeating steps 10–11 to finish the fabric edge on the opposite side, consider where you want to position the chain and how long you want it to be.

## 13. Trim the chain

Fold the fabric on the unfinished end over and lay the chain at least ½" (1.5cm) over from the fabric's edge. Use the flush cutters to trim the chain as needed, making sure to leave at least 2" (5cm) for attaching to the board.

## 14. Finish the end and attach the chain

Repeat steps 10–11 for the I side. As you complete step 11, add glue to the chain and fold the fabric over it. Allow the glue to dry thoroughly.

If desired, use the lint brush to pick up and stray fibers from the black background.

# BOGUS BILLIARD

Fun fact: the Internet age, while entertaining us all with videos of kittens, has made pool hustling practically extinct. Nowadays if a fish gets taken by a sand-bagging shark with a sneaky Pete, he doesn't just cry in his beer. He pulls out his smartphone and blows the whistle on the hustler's alias, appearance and moves. After that, a poor shark just might have to go legit.

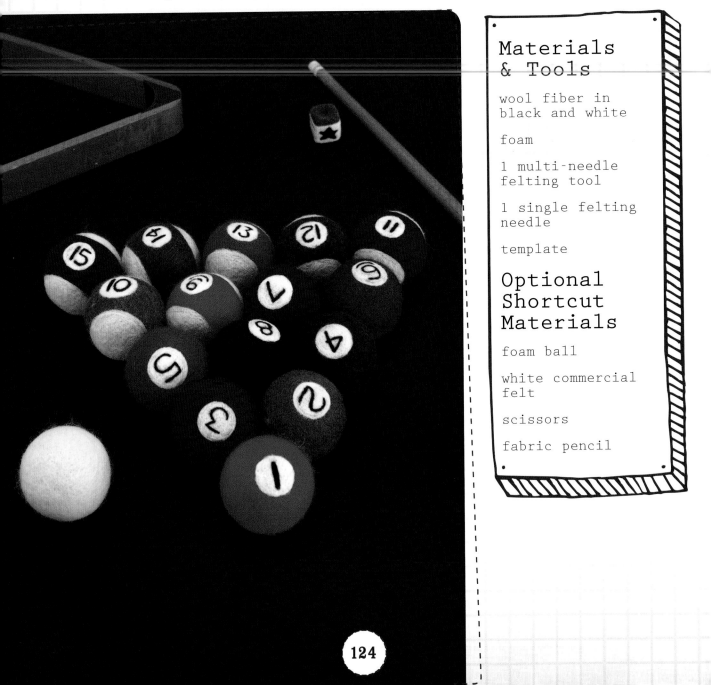

## Materials & Tools

wool fiber in black and white

foam

1 multi-needle felting tool

1 single felting needle

template

## Optional Shortcut Materials

foam ball

white commercial felt

scissors

fabric pencil

## 1. Make and prep the ball

Using black fiber and a single felting needle, create a ball from scratch or around a foam base about 2¼" (5.5cm) in diameter (see Felt a Ball on page 17 or Soft Objects on page 27). Use the fabric pencil to trace or freehand a circle. (I did mine freehand, adding the 8 in the middle to make sure the circle was a good size.)

## 2. Add the detail

Use a small tuft of white fiber or cut a piece of white commercial felt to size to make the white circle (see Embellishing on page 29). Add very thin wisps of black fiber to the circle to form the 8. If free-forming the 8 doesn't sound fun, use a fabric pencil to draw it on first and felt along the lines.

**Tip** *If you want to make a whole set of billiard balls, the stripey ones actually start with a ball in the stripe color. The white circles on each side of the stripe get felted on after.*

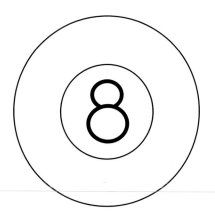

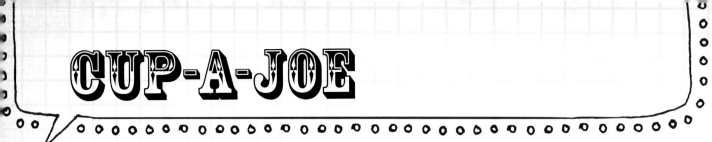

# CUP-A-JOE

Coffee isn't just a beverage that comes from a bean. Coffee is food, a reason for being, a facilitator of genius and the grease on the wheels of everyday chitchat. They name shops after it, write songs about it, plan events around it and make brilliant refined machines to get the very best of it into your cup. This country, among others, was built on coffee and there is no way this book would exist without it. Anyway … (sigh) … I love coffee. Grab your favorite mug to model for this project.

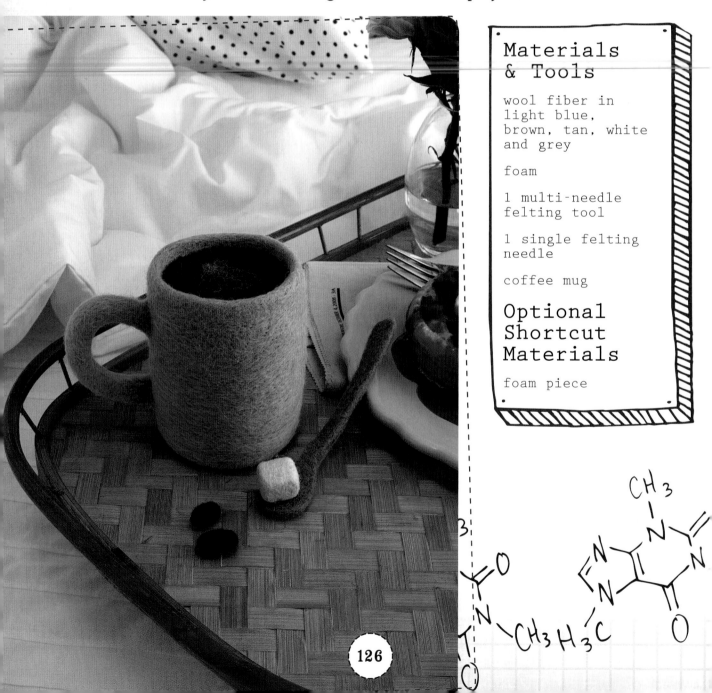

## Materials & Tools

wool fiber in light blue, brown, tan, white and grey

foam

1 multi-needle felting tool

1 single felting needle

coffee mug

## Optional Shortcut Materials

foam piece

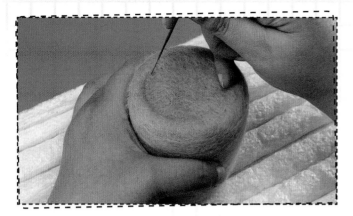

## 1. Make a cup base

Get out your favorite coffee mug and study its shape and size. Use a single needle and light blue fiber to build the body of the mug from scratch or around a piece of foam (see 3D Part I: Shapes on page 17 or Soft Objects on page 27), referring to your mug as you build the felt mug. After the cup has started to take shape but before it gets too solid, use extra pokes at the bottom to flatten it out. Use extra pokes from the top down to create a divot where the coffee will eventually go. Add wisps of fiber as needed to build up the rim of the mug.

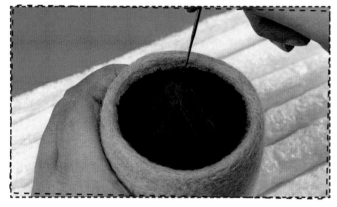

## 2. Add the coffee

Add a tuft of brown fiber to the inside of the mug to make it look full of delicious life-giving java (see Embellishing on page 29). Add a few wisps of tan and white for *café au lait* swirls.

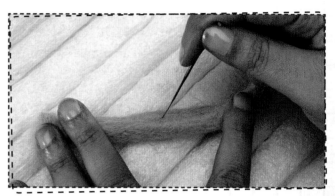

## 3. Make a handle

Use light blue fiber to make a log with both ends fuzzy (see Felt a Log on page 21). Poke more on one side of the log to give the handle a flat inside edge. Add fiber as needed to thicken and strengthen the handle, leaving both ends fuzzy.

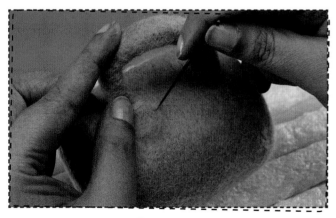

## 4. Attach the handle

When you finish shaping it, felt the fuzzy ends into the side of the mug until secure. Attach the handle to the bottom of the mug first. Arch the handle and hold the opposite end to the cup so the handle angles slightly up. Attach the top of the handle to the cup.

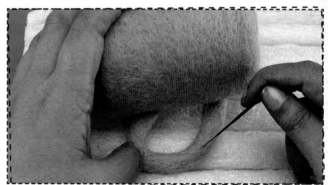

## 5. Refine the handle

Lay the handle onto the foam and, while gently bending the handle toward the top of the cup, poke along the edges to solidify the shape. Flip and poke as needed from all sides to finish shaping the handle.

## 6. Shape the sugar cube

Use a tuft of white fiber to make a loosely felted ball. Use tiny shallow pokes on the ball to flatten the sides and create the cube shape. (Note: Always use foam under your felting. This is pictured without foam for photo purposes only.)

## 7. Finish the cube

Add thin wisps of fiber to the cube as needed to thicken the sugar as you continue to use shallow pokes on each side of the cube.

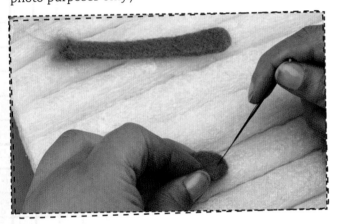

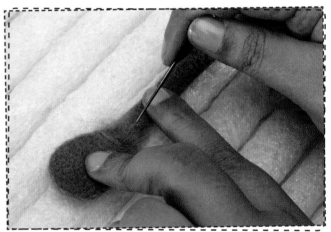

## 8. Make spoon parts

Use a tuft of grey fiber to make a long flat log. Add fiber to the handle end to make it wider and round off the end. Leave the other end fuzzy. For the head of the spoon, separately felt a small oblong piece with grey fiber, rounded and thinner on one side, fuzzy on the other.

## 9. Connect the spoon parts

Poke the fuzzy end of the handle to the fuzzy part of the spoon head (see Forming Attachments on page 23). Add thin wisps of grey to the connection point to strengthen the neck of the spoon. You can add another thin layer of fiber and poke it in all over the spoon to give it a clean finish.

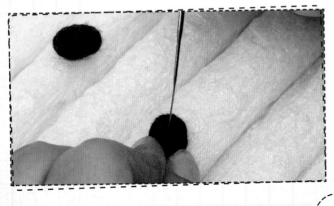

## 10. Make beans

Use the brown fiber to make the beans, rounded on one side and flat on the other (see 3D Part I: Shapes on page 17). Use extra pokes down the center of the flat side to make an indent.

# TILT A WALL

Perhaps one of the only activities that can be considered as genuinely enjoyable as needle felting is pinball. I am by no means a Pinball Wizard, but I have plenty of witnesses to verify that I am, indeed, Special When Lit.

## Materials & Tools

wool fiber in white, orange, yellow, red and grey

foam

1 single felting needle

templates

hanging device

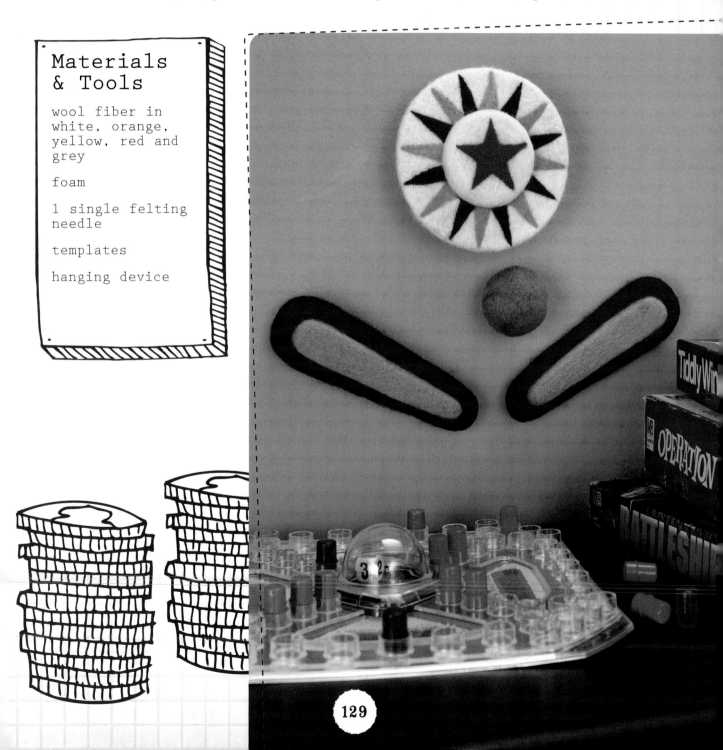

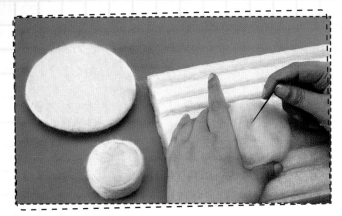

## 1. Make the bumper pieces

Using the templates as your guide, use white fiber and a single needle to make the three bumper pieces. The largest piece is about ⅛" (3mm) thick. The top piece is a smaller, thicker puck, about ¼" (6mm) thick, with rounded edges. Use the single needle to attach the top piece to the large one. The final piece will go on the back of the large one a little later, and will measure about ½" (1.5cm) thick.

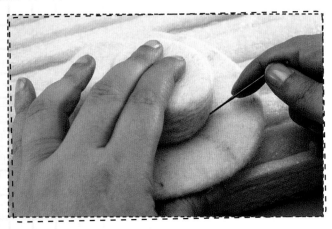

## 3. Add the back piece

Use a single needle to attach the third puck you made to the bottom of the bumper. This will help make the whole thing stick out from the wall like a real bumper when hung.

**Tip** *If freehanding the spike design doesn't seem fun to you, use the template by tracing it onto the piece, or cutting it out and pinning and felting in the spaces like a stencil.*

## 2. Detail the bumper

Use the template or freehand the star design onto the top of the bumper with orange fiber, working in small tufts (see Embellishing on page 29). For the spike design, start by felting one long thin triangle onto the main disc with red fiber and a single needle, lining it up with the top point of the orange star. Make a second red triangle directly across the disc on the opposite side. If the disc were a clock, these triangles would be at 12 and 6. Make two more red triangles, this time at 9 and 3. Then make 4 more red triangles, centering each one between a pair of the first ones. Finally, add a yellow triangle centered between each pair of red triangles until the design is complete.

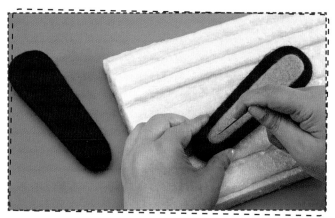

## 4. Make the flippers

Use red fiber and a single felting needle to felt the base of the flippers, flat on the top and bottom with rounded edges all the way around. Measure against the template to get the right size and shape. Add layers of fiber to thicken the shape. Add yellow fiber to the top in small tufts to create the top detail of the bumper, which will also be flat on the top and rounded on the edges.

## 5. Make the ball

Use the grey fiber to felt a big round pinball of joy (see Felt a Ball on page 17).

**Tip**

*You can use your favorite method of art hanging for these pieces. I use adhesive hook-and-eye strips because it works and I don't care about the paint on my walls.*

Templates have been reduced by 75 percent. Enlarge the images as needed.

# WIENER PLANT, PASTILLUM BOTELLO FARTUM

When we were kids, my sister was obsessed with hot dogs. Sure, she liked to eat them, but mostly she thought they were hilarious. She could make herself laugh out loud for hours merely by adding the words "hot" and "dog" to her favorite songs. It's no surprise that even though she's all grown up, this project was her idea.

## Materials & Tools

wool fiber in dark green, light green, brown, tan, white, rust, red and yellow

craft wire or pipe cleaner

foam

1 multi-needle felting tool

1 single felting needles

## Optional Shortcut Materials

foam piece

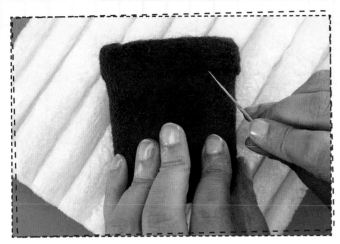

## 1. Make the pot

Use a single needle and dark green fiber to build the body of the pot from scratch or around a piece of foam (see 3D Part I: Shapes on page 17 or Soft Objects on page 27). Add layers of fiber to create thickness, making the bottom more narrow than the top. Once the pot has started to take shape but before it gets too solid, use extra pokes at the bottom to flatten it out. Use extra pokes from the top down to create a divot where the dirt will eventually go. Add tufts of fiber as needed to build up the rim of the pot, poking from the top and the sides.

## 2. Add the dirt

Add a tuft of brown fiber to the inside of the pot to make it nice and dirty.

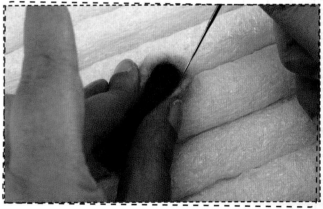

## 4. Attach the pieces

Place the wiener inside the bun and felt around its edges, tucking it into the bun nice and snuggly.

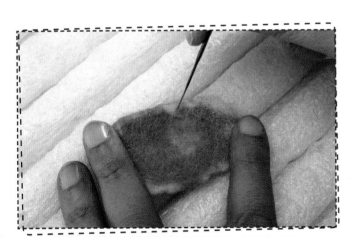

## 3. Make the bun and hot dog

Use the rust fiber to make a log with rounded ends. Mix some tan and white fiber together for the bun. Make a flat piece of felt in a long oval shape.

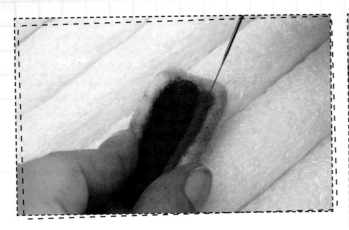

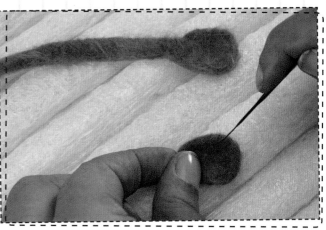

## 5. Add condiments

Poke a thin wisp of yellow on one side of the wiener and a thin wisp of red on the other to make mustard and ketchup.

## 6. Make large stem

Use light green fiber and craft wire to create the long stem (see Making An Armature on page 35). Add light green fiber to one end of the stem and poke it into a flat oblong leaf shape with a rounded top. Leave the other end of the stem fuzzy. Separately felt another flat oblong leaf piece with light green fiber, rounded on one side, fuzzy on the other.

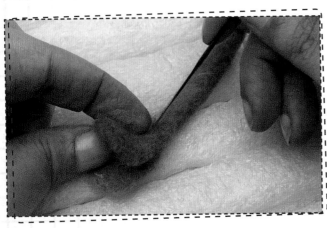

## 7. Connect the pieces

Connect the fuzzy end of the leaf to the stem at the base of the leaf that's already there to make an opening bud. Wrap a bit of light green fiber around the base of the bud to smooth and secure it to the stem.

## 8. Add the wiener

Place the completed hot dog's end into the open bud and felt it from all sides to secure it into place.

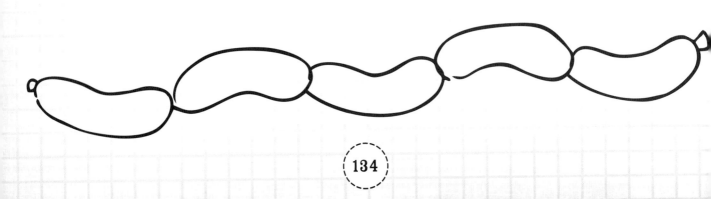

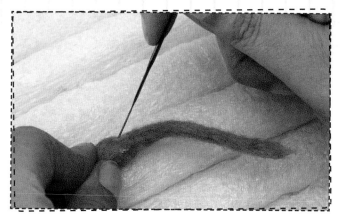

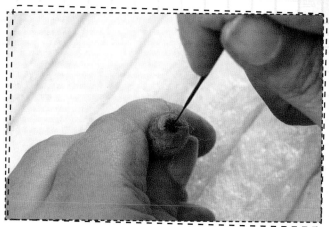

## 9. Make the second stem

Repeat the process in step 6 to create a second, smaller stem, this time wrapping a small tuft of light green fiber to the top of the stem to create the barely-opening bud.

## 10. Add a wiener bud

Poke a tiny bit of rust fiber into the center of the second smaller bud, and a bit of tan and white fiber around it to make the beginnings of a burgeoning wiener.

## 11. Attach the stems

Poke the fuzzy end of the smaller stem into the center of the dirt. Poke the fuzzy end of the larger stem into the dirt close to the first stem but closer to the edge of the pot.

## 12. Finishing touch

Finally, take a little tuft of light green fiber and felt a small nub into the dirt a little closer to the edge of the pot to create a brand new baby sprout signifying the freshness of the hot dogs to come. It's lunch time, get yourself a hot dog.

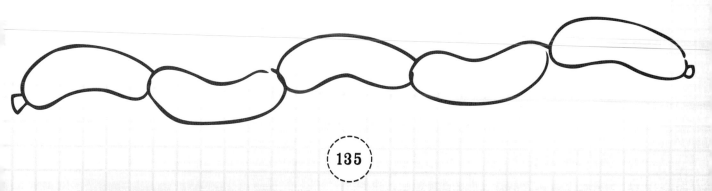

# RETRO KITSCHEN WALL ART

Do people still have those giant wooden forks and spoons hanging on their kitchen wall? I like to think they are popular because people don't trust you to know that you're standing in the kitchen and might, therefore, wee in the sink in total confusion. I prefer this mid-century utensil, made as an homage to Sy Greenblum and Spatula City. (They're open 'till midnight!)

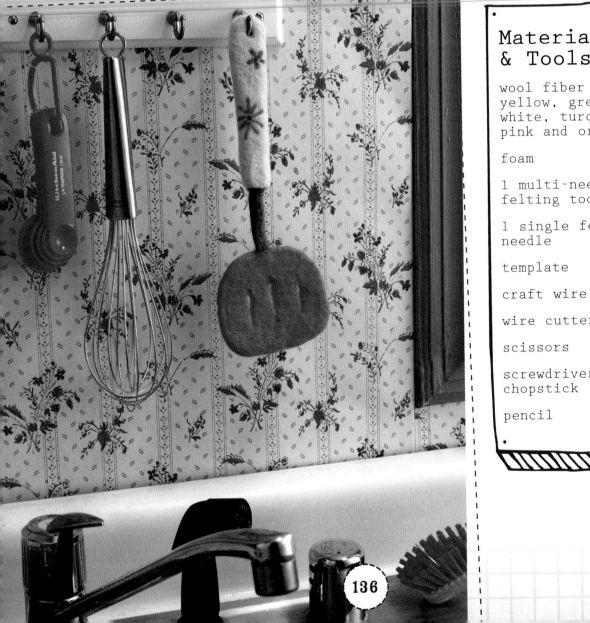

## Materials & Tools

wool fiber in yellow, grey, white, turquoise, pink and orange

foam

1 multi-needle felting tool

1 single felting needle

template

craft wire

wire cutters

scissors

screwdriver or chopstick

pencil

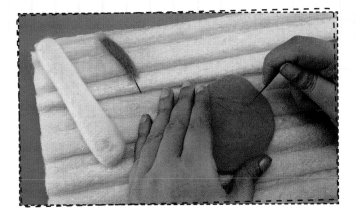

## 1. Make the pieces

For the flipper end, use yellow fiber to create a small round patch of flat felt (see Creating Flat Fabric on page 13). Use the template to measure the size and shape of the flipper. As it thickens, use a single needle to felt around the edges to achieve the desired shape. For the neck, use grey fiber and craft wire to create a flat piece with rounded edges and fuzzy ends (see Making an Armature on page 25). Leave about ¼" (6mm) of wire on each end of the grey piece. For the handle, use white fiber and a single felting needle to create a thick log, flat on each side and rounded on the edges. Add more fiber toward the base of the handle to make it bigger and round it off. Use a single needle to make the opposite end of the handle smaller and smooth down the fuzzy. Use the template as needed to create the desired shape and size.

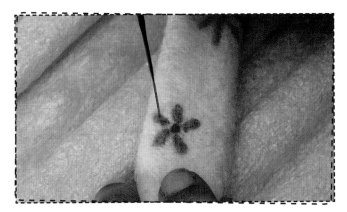

## 2. Add details

Use tiny wisps of yellow and pink to make the flower petals, and use a tiny bit of turquoise and orange for the center of the flowers (see Embellishing on page 29).

## 3. Start a hole

Using small, sharp scissors, carefully push the tip of the scissor blade into the base of the handle about ½" (1.5cm) from the bottom.

## 4. Widen the hole

Use a screwdriver or chopstick to push through the cut you made with the scissors to stretch it and make it more pronounced.

## 5. Clean up the hole

Use a single needle around the outside and inner edge of the hole to neaten any loose fibers and make the hole more stable.

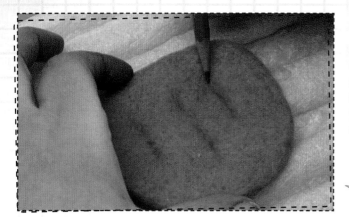

## 6. Prep the flipper

Use a pencil to mark the straight, thin vertical rectangle at the center of the flipper piece, about 1¼" (3cm) long. Make two more rectangles, one on each side of the first. They should start at the same top point of the center line, but stop about ⅛" (3mm) short of the bottom.

**Tip** *If freehanding the flipper lines doesn't seem fun to you, use the template by tracing it onto the piece, or cutting it out and pinning and felting in the spaces like a stencil.*

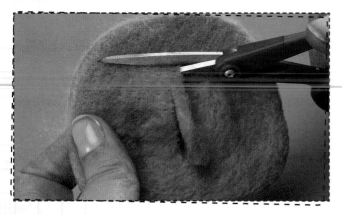

## 7. Cut out the rectangle

Fold the flipper felt in half. Use the scissors to make a small cut on the middle vertical line. Insert the scissors into the hole you made and carefully cut out the rectangle along the drawn line.

## 8. Refine the rectangles

Repeat steps 6–7 for the other two rectangle cutouts. Use a single needle to tidy or tighten up the cut edges as needed.

## 9. Attach the neck

Push one end of the wire into the thin end of the handle and poke in the fuzzy grey fiber to connect the two pieces (see Forming Attachments on page 23).

## 10. Secure the neck

Add tiny wisps of grey to the attachment spot and poke them into both the handle and the neck piece as needed for strength.

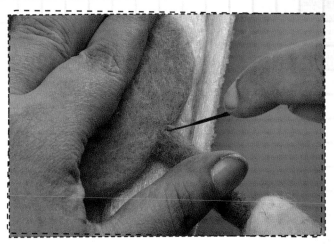

## 11. Attach the flipper

Push the other end of the neck wire into the center of the flipper.

## 12. Secure the flipper

Use a single felting needle to felt the fuzzy grey fiber into place to secure the flipper.

**Tip** *If some of the grey fiber shows through at the base of the flipper, add some tiny yellow wisps and poke them into place as a cover-up.*

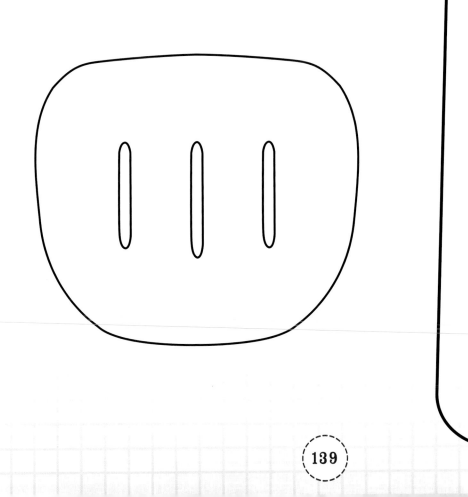

# YOU ARE HERE

Let's say you are driving down the street, lost and confused and seeking help from a passerby. You pull up next to a clearly fantastic and friendly woman who turns out to be me. "Can you tell me how to find the place I'm trying to go?" you might ask. I will turn with a knowing glance and a wide smile and say "Uh ... heh ...(cough)" and beg off, allowing you to believe that I'm not a native English speaker. I don't do this because I'm unkind, but because I'm lucky to find my way home from my studio every day. Therefore, bow down before this magnified map icon. It is my master.

## Materials & Tools

wool fiber in rose and black

foam

1 multi-needle felting tool

1 single felting needle

## 1. Make two pieces

Use rose fiber to make a large piece of flat felt (see Creating Flat Fabric on page 13). Place extra layers around the edge of the fabric to make it round. Add and poke a few more layers creating a good start to a thick, round puck, approximately 9" (23cm) in diameter.

For the triangle, use rose fiber to make a piece of flat felt. This time, instead of adding fiber in the round, fold the ends of the rectangle toward the center creating a triangle shape and poke it into place, approximately 4½" (11.cm) at the wide base and about 6½" (16.5cm) long. Add and poke more fiber until the triangle is about the same thickness and texture as the circle.

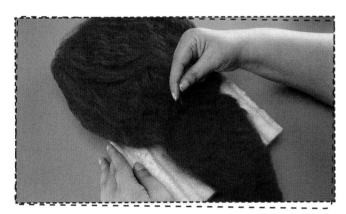

## 2. Attach the pieces

Use a single needle to attach the fuzzy end of the triangle to one side of the circle.

## 3. Build bulk

Continue adding and poking more and more layers of tufts. Lay out and poke in the tufts of fiber on one side, then repeat the process on the other side. Allow some of the fiber to overlap the edges, wrap it under the piece and felt it into place.

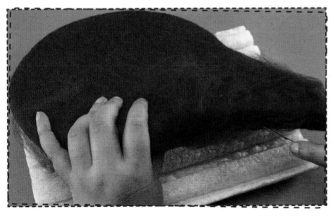

## 4. Shape it up

Once the piece begins to thicken and hold its shape, work it around the edges to flatten them into a puck form, at least 1¼" (3cm) thick. Repeat steps 3 and 4 as needed until you reach the desired thickness and shape.

## 5. Add details

Use long thin wisps of black fiber and a single felting needle to create a continuous line around the outside edge of the piece (see Make a Stripe, Straight Up on page 29). Use a tuft of black to make a large polka dot in the center of the round shape (see Poke-a-Dot, Flat and Fine on page 33). You are now officially "here."

# RESOURCES

## ADDITIONAL CONTENT
**Wall Tapestry Templates**
more great drawings available for download from artist, animator, cat lover Demian Parker
www.villainmachine.com/feltingfun

## SUPPLIES
**Hi-Fiber**
wool fiber, needles, eco-friendly foam, kits and more
hifiberkits.com

**Compilation of various suppliers**
members.peak.org/~spark/feltsources.html

## BATTS AND SPECIAL FIBER

**Loop**
loop.etsy.com

**ArtClub**
harveyvilleproject.com/artclub/

**Spun Right Round**
spunrightround.etsy.com

**Holly EQQ**
hollyeqq.com

**Nikki Wheeler**
handmade wool felt fabric and hand dyed roving
nikkiwheeler.etsy.com

## MISC. MATERIALS
**Cowgirl Snaps**
awesome assortments of snaps and snap tools
www.etsy.com/shop/CowgirlSnaps

**Creation Station**
endlessly fabulous surplus and recycled goodies
creationstationinc.com

**FilzFelt**
extra thick commercial felt
filzfelt.etsy.com

**Felt Craft Studio**
beautiful all wool commercial felt
feltcraftstudio.etsy.com

**K & J Magnetics, Inc.**
all the magnets you could want
kjmagnetics.com

**Seattle Fabrics Online**
grommets and grommet tools
www.seattlefabrics.com/gromsnap.html

**Yo-Yo Guy**
string, info and other yo-yo goodies
www.yoyoguy.com

## INSPIRATION, INFORMATION AND COMMUNITY:
**I Felt Awesome**
a place to share photos of the projects you make from the book
www.ifeltawesome.com

**Flickr Needle Felting Group**
flickr.com/groups/needlefelting

**Felting Forum**
feltingforum.com

**Fiber Arts Magazine**
fiberarts.com

## STUFF I LOVE
During the making of this book, I …

**found creative inspiration on:**
Make + Meaning: makeandmeaning.com
43 Folders: 43folders.com
CraftyPod: craftypod.com
Craft Magazine: blog.craftzine.com
Mr X Stitch: mrxstitch.com

**listened to the music of:**
Jonathan Coulton, Talking Heads, Richard Cheese, The Who, Paul McCartney, ELO, Ed's Redeeming Qualities, Mirah, The Tiger Lillies, Roosevelt Franklin, Harry Nilsson, Elvis Costello, Frankie Lymon, Nellie McKay, The Jam, Larry Gallagher, The Kinks

**listened to these podcasts:**
You Look Nice Today, Wiretap, Radiolab, The Moth, This American Life, WTF with Mark Maron

**used these applications:**
OmniGraffle, OmniFocus, Birdhouse, Harvest

**played these games:**
Plants vs Zombies, Peggle, Bubble Town, Angry Birds

**consumed a lot of:**
Talking Rain Sparkling Water, 16 oz. quadruple ice lattes (with extra ice) from Short Stop Coffee

# INDEX

# GET MORE FIBER

## SWEET NEEDLE FELTS

### By Jenn Docherty

*Sweet Needle Felts* features all the techniques and information you will need to begin needle felting, including step-by-step instructions for 25 adorable projects. Learn how to create wearable items such as jewelry, scarves, hats and bags. Decorate your home with cozy pillows and rugs. Needle felt huggable, lovable dolls and toys. Using just a few simple tools, turn soft, warm wool into colorful creations to wear, give and hug!

ISBN 13: 978-1-60061-039-4
ISBN 10: 1-60061-039-0
paperback, 128 pages, Z1490

## ME MAKE MONSTER

### By Jenny Harada

In *Me Make Monster*, Jenny Harada presents a hoard of funky monster projects so ugly they're cute. Bring to life your own fantastic brood as you follow step-by-step instructions to create a true mish mash of monsterdom—18 monster in all! Everything from plush huggable beasties and a furry pillow cover to a fanged fiendish trinket box and google-eyed dice. Whatever kind of monster may tickle your fancy (or your feet) you'll find one of his breed to spawn and love.

ISBN 13: 978-1-60061-863-5
ISBN 10: 1-60061-863-4
paperback, 144 pages, Z5431

## STRAY SOCK SEWING, TOO

### By Daniel

Make friends with your socks! Every sock you have has the potential to be your new best friend with a little help from *Stray Sock Sewing, Too*. Inside, clear step-by-step instructions teach you the basics of sewing. Then you'll learn to create fourteen unique characters including The Wise Owl, Happy Monkey and Cheshire Cat. Your socks will never be the same once you try your hand at *Stray Sock Sewing, Too!*

ISBN 13: 978-1-60061-907-6
ISBN 10: 1-60061-907-X
paperback, 144 pages, Z5760

These and other fine North Light titles are available at your local craft retailer, bookstore or online supplier, or visit our website at www.mycraftivitystore.com.